الرَّحْمٰنِ الرَّحِيْمِ

The Children's Book of Ṣalāh

Ghulam Sarwar

The Muslim Educational Trust

ISBN 0 907261 09 4

1st Edition, March 1984 (10,000)
2nd Edition, October 1987 (12,000)
3rd Revised Edition, October 1990 (12,000)
3rd Revised Edition, Reprinted July 1993 (15,000)
3rd Revised Edition, Reprinted January 1996 (15,000)

Published by
The Muslim Educational Trust
130 Stroud Green Road
London N4 3RZ, UK
Tel: 0171 272 8502
Fax: 0171 281 3457

British Library Cataloguing in Publication Data
Sarwar, Ghulam
The Children's Book of Ṣalāh
1. *Prayer (Islām) – Juvenile literature*
I. *Title*
297'.43 *BP178*

ISBN 0 907261 09 4

Printed and bound in Great Britain by
Midland Regional Printers
Jubilee House
Nottingham Road
Nottingham NG7 7BT

Contents

		Page
	Preface to 1st Edition	4
	Transliteration	6
1	**Aṣ-Ṣalāh** : Meaning & Importance, Purpose, 'Ibādah and Aṣ-Ṣalāh and Jihād, Names and Timings of Aṣ-Ṣalāh	7
2	**Preparation for Aṣ-Ṣalāh** : Ṭahārah, Essentials of Aṣ-Ṣalāh, Ghusl, Wuḍū', Tayammum, Adhān, Iqāmah	11
3	**Details of Aṣ-Ṣalāh** : Kinds, Farā'id, Wājibāt, Sunnah, Farḍ Raka'hs, Chart of Aṣ-Ṣalāh	19
4	**How to Perform Aṣ-Ṣalāh** : Step 1 to Step 11, Ṣalātul Witr and Sajdatus Sahw, Du'ā'	24
5	**Aṣ-Ṣalāh on Special Occasions** : Ṣalātul Jumu'ah, Ṣalātul Janāzah, Ṣalātul 'Idain, Ṣalātul Musāfir, Ṣalātul Istikhārah, Qaḍā' of Aṣ-Ṣalāh, Lessons of Aṣ-Ṣalāh	34
6	**Eleven Surahs of the Qur'ān**	42
7	**Selected Verses from the Qur'ān on Ma'rūf and Munkar**	49
8	**Declaration of Faith : Ash-Shahādah** : Five Kalimahs	54
	Appendix I — Islamic Books for Schools	56
	Appendix II — Muslim Journals in English	59
	Appendix III — Muslim Bookshops in the U.K.	60
	Appendix IV — Major Publishers of Islamic Books	61
	Select Bibliography	63

Preface to 1st Edition

The future of a community depends on how its young generation is educated and brought up. Young people of today are the leaders of tomorrow. They will shoulder the future responsibilities which the community have to discharge as a part of the dynamic and quickly shrinking world in which they live.

The question of disseminating the universal message of Islām in the West is integrally linked with the Islamic orientation of the English-speaking young Muslims. This is by no means an easy task. It is a daunting challenge. The Muslim Educational Trust has been trying its best under the given circumstances and within available resources to meet this challenge. The achievements are modest. We bow our heads down to Allāh in praise. The credit for the achievements of His slaves rightly and justly belongs to Him.

Aṣ-Ṣalāh is one of the fundamental duties of Islām. It is the foundation of *'Ībādah*, the sum total of all human activities performed to gain Allāh's pleasure. Prophet Muḥammad (Peace be upon him) said, "Aṣ-Ṣalāh is the key to paradise." Indeed, in the constant and conscious performance of this obligatory duty lies the success of believers. Allāh, our Merciful and loving Creator, says : *"Successful are the believers who are humble in their prayers."* (Sūratul Mu'minūn 23 : 1-2)

I have been thinking for some time to write a book on *Aṣ-Ṣalāh* for English-speaking young Muslims in easy language in order to acquaint them with the basic details of how to perform it. The result is *The Children's Book of Ṣalāh*. I am humbled by the mercy of Almighty Allāh who enabled me to materialise my thinking. My success is for the readers to judge. Responsibility for all errors and mistakes is unquestionably mine. I would gratefully appreciate any comments.

I have arranged the topics to learn in a systematic way beginning with the meaning and importance of *Aṣ-Ṣalāh*. I have added at the end a chapter on *Ma'rūf* (Right) and *Munkar* (Wrong). I hope regular performance of *Aṣ-Ṣalāh* will inspire young Muslims to work for the establishment of *Ma'rūf* in a society and the eradication of *Munkar*.

I urge parents and teachers to take special care in teaching the correct pronunciation of various Islamic terms and names used in the performance of *Aṣ-Ṣalāh*. I believe, given the will, it is not difficult.

I must point out here that the theoretical teaching of *Aṣ-Ṣalāh* by parents and teachers can be effective only if they practice it themselves. Many of us these days moan about growing children who are drifting away from the teachings of Islām. It will help if we can set up examples for our children since *examples are better than precepts*; in the case of *Aṣ-Ṣalāh* this is more than true.

May Allāh accept my humble efforts and make it a source of my salvation in the life after death.

Wa mā tawfīqī illā billāh. [Surāh Hūd 11 : 88 (And my success in my task can only come from Allāh.)]

London
Jumāda Al-Thānī, 1404 AH
March, 1984 CE.

Ghulam Sarwar

Note to the Third Revised Edition

Alḥamdullillāh (All praise is for Allāh), the second edition of my book *'The Children's Book of Ṣalāh'* was sold out in a shorter time than I expected. The third edition is now before the readers. It has been thoroughly revised and the errors, especially in the Arabic, have been corrected. I hope the book will continue to receive the same support as before from teachers, parents, pupils and booksellers.

May Allāh accept my humble efforts, Āmin!

Rabī' Al-Awwal 1411 AH
October, 1990 CE

Ghulam Sarwar

Transliteration

Correct pronunciation of Arabic words is very important. Care and attention are needed in training young people to pronounce Arabic correctly.

Transliteration marks have been shown below as a guide to correct pronunciation. These marks help to show how the words should sound but it is not possible to show on a printed page exactly how to pronounce words.

For example, the word *Allāh* cannot be pronounced correctly unless the two *Ls* are sounded distinctly, and the last *A* is a long sound. The name *Muḥammad* should be pronounced with a glottal sound of *H* rather than the normal *H* sound.

Ideally, it is best to listen to an Arabic-speaking person, or someone who has learned how to say Arabic words correctly. A tape-recording or record can alşo help.

Arabic letter	*Transliteration sign*	*Example*	*Arabic letter*	*Transliteration sign*	*Example*
ء	'	Malā'ikah	ط	ṭ	Lūṭ
ـَا	ā	Dāwūd	ظ	ẓ	Ẓuhr
ـُو	ū	Dāwūd	ع	‘	‘Īsā
ـِي	ī	Khadījah	غ	gh	Maghrib
ب	b	Bilāl	ف	f	Fāṭimah
ت	t	Tirmidhī	ق	q	Fārūq
ث	th	‘Uthmān	ك	k	Mikā'īl
ج	J	Jannah	ل	l	Allāh
ح	ḥ	Muḥammad	م	m	Mūsā
خ	kh	Khalīfah	ن	n	Nūḥ
د	d	Dāwūd	و	w	Ṣawm
ذ	dh	Tirmidhī	ه ه	h	Ibrāhīm
ر	r	Raḥmān	ة (silent)	h	Ṣalāh
ز	z	Zakāh	ى	y	Yāsīn
س	s	‘Īsā	ـَوْ	aw	Yawmuddīn
ش	sh	Shahādah	ـَيْ	ai	Sulaimān
ص	ṣ	Ṣawm	ـِيَّ	iyy	Zakariyyā
ض	ḍ	Ramaḍān	ـَوَّ	aww	Awwāl

Aṣ-Ṣalāh : اَلصَّلَاةُ :- 1

Aṣ-Ṣalāh : Its Meaning and Importance

Islām is a complete way of life. It is the system of life which Allāh has chosen for all mankind. The Qur'ān says, *"Surely, the way of life acceptable to Allāh is Islām."* (Sūrah Āli 'Imrān 3 : 19) Islām is the guidance (Hidayah) for all affairs of life. It is based on five basic duties known as the pillars of Islām (Arkānul Islām). The first of these is *Ash-Shahādah* — the declaration of faith. This declaration is at the centre of all Islamic duties. *Ash-Shahādah* is testifying that *there is no god but Allāh and Muḥammad is the messenger of Allāh.* As soon as a person freely testifies this, he becomes a Muslim. He now has to do certain specific duties, one of which is *Aṣ-Ṣalāh*, known as the second pillar of Islām. Besides *Ash-Shahādah* and *Aṣ-Ṣalāh*, the three other basic duties are *Az-Zakāh* (Welfare Contribution), *Aṣ-Ṣawm* (Fasting in the month of Ramaḍān) and *Al-Ḥajj* (Pilgrimage to Makkah).

Aṣ-Ṣalāh (known also as Namaz, which is a Persian word) is the most important of all acts of worship *('Ibādah). Aṣ-Ṣalāh* is the prayer offered to Allāh by specific words and actions as shown by Prophet Muḥammad (Peace be upon him).

It is very difficult to translate *Aṣ-Ṣalāh* into English. The nearest English words are 'prayer', 'blessings', 'supplication' or 'grace'. The word prayer can mean any sort of prayer but, in Islām, *Aṣ-Ṣalāh* is the prescribed prayer which has to be offered in a particular way at set times. It is better to use the Arabic word *Aṣ-Ṣalāh* at all times.

Aṣ-Ṣalāh is a practical sign of our faith (Īmān) in Allāh and Islām. It differentiates a believer from one who does not believe (Kafir). That is why Allāh commanded *"Guard strictly your Ṣalāh, especially the middle Ṣalāh and stand before Allāh with all devotion."* (Sūratul Baqarah 2 : 238) *Aṣ-Ṣalāh* helps us to be good, well behaved, disciplined, modest and successful. Prophet Muḥammad (Pbuh) said, "The first thing that the slave of Allāh will be called upon to account for on the day of judgement will be Aṣ-Ṣalāh. If it was good, his actions will be taken as good; if it was bad, his actions will be taken as bad." Allāh says in the *Qur'ān, "Surely,*

Ṣalāh keeps you away from indecency and evil." (Sūratul 'Ankabūt 29 : 45) You should start to say *Aṣ-Ṣalāh* when you are seven years old. You must be regular in saying your *Aṣ-Ṣalāh* when you are ten years old.

Make it a point to understand the importance of *Aṣ-Ṣalāh* and make a promise to offer it daily at fixed times.

Purpose of Aṣ-Ṣalāh

It is important to make *Aṣ-Ṣalāh* a part of your life. The *Qur'ān* commands us to establish *Aṣ-Ṣalāh* (Aqīmuṣ Ṣalāh). It signifies that Allāh commands us to perform *Aṣ-Ṣalāh* and ask others to do the same. We are not alone; we belong to the society of mankind. *Aṣ-Ṣalāh* prepares society as well as each of us to obey the Laws of Allāh.

The purpose of establishing *Aṣ-Ṣalāh* is to remember Allāh (Dhikrullāh). Allāh commands in the *Qur'ān : "Establish Aṣ-Ṣalāh to remember Me."* (Sūrah Ṭāhā 20; 14) To remember Allāh means to obey Him in all affairs of life.

After testifying *Ash-Shahādah*, Muslims must be ready to say *Aṣ-Ṣalāh*. This is the first sign of their testimony. It means they are prepared to act on this testimony. This is why in Islām words and actions must go together. We must do what we say. Otherwise, our words are meaningless.

Aṣ-Ṣalāh must affect our life-style. It must inspire us to obey Allāh in every way. If our *Aṣ-Ṣalāh* does not improve our behaviour, we must think carefully and find out where we are going wrong.

'Ibādah and Aṣ-Ṣalāh

'Ibādah, an Arabic word, means worship and obedience to Allāh. Allāh says in the *Qur'ān : "Indeed I created Jinn and human-beings for no other purpose but to worship Me."* (Sūrat-udh-Dhariyāt 51 : 56) Everything we do is *'Ibādah*, if we do it for Allāh's sake. For example, obeying parents, respecting elders, eating Ḥalāl food, telling the truth and not telling lies, keeping promises, controlling greed, helping the poor and the needy and honesty in trade and politics are all acts of *'Ibādah*. Our purpose in life is to seek Allāh's pleasure through *'Ibādah* and *Aṣ-Ṣalāh* prepares us to achieve this.

Four of the basic duties of Islām —*Aṣ-Ṣalāh, Az-Zakāh, Aṣ-Ṣawm* and *Al-Ḥajj* — are the main forms of *'Ibādah*. Performance of these duties prepares us to obey the commands of Allāh in all affairs of our life. *Aṣ-Ṣalāh* is the most important of these four basic duties. It brings us closer to our Creator. It trains us to obey Him. Allāh, our Creator, is happy and pleased when we obey His commands. He in return gives us peace and happiness in this life and in the life hereafter (Ākhirah).

Aṣ-Ṣalāh and Jihād

Jihād means doing one's utmost to see that *Ma'rūf*(Right) is established in a society and *Munkar* (Wrong) is removed from it. *'Ibādah* should prepare us for *Jihād* in the way of Allāh. Our *'Ibādah* is meaningful if it leads us to work for the cause of Allāh. *Aṣ-Ṣalāh* is for *'Ibādah* and *'Ibādah* is for *Jihād fī sabī lillāh* (Jihād in the way of Allāh).

You have learned before that Islām is the complete way of life chosen by Allāh for mankind. In Islām, human life is a unit. One aspect of life is related to another. For instance, the declaration of faith *(Ash-Shahādah)* leads to the performance of the other basic duties : *Aṣ-Ṣalāh, Az-Zakāh, Aṣ-Ṣawm* and *Al-Ḥajj*. These duties prepare us for *Jihād fī sabī lillāh*.

Our life does not end with death. The real and permanent life is the life after death. So, we must work for the success in the never-ending life. There will be a test on the *day of judgement* when all our actions in this life will be judged by Allāh. One who succeeds will be rewarded by Paradise *(Al-Jannah)*, a place of permanent happiness and joy, and the one who fails will face torment in Hell *(Jahannam)*, a place of terrible suffering and pain. *Jihād fī sabī lillāh* is the surest way to success in the life after death.

Names of Aṣ-Ṣalāh

A Muslim must offer *Aṣ-Ṣalāh* five times a day. These five daily *Ṣalāh* are :

1 **Ṣalātul Fajr** (Dawn Prayer) — صَلَاةُ الْفَجْرِ

2 **Ṣalātuẓ Ẓuhr** (After Mid-day Prayer) — صَلَاةُ الظُّهْرِ

3 **Ṣalātul 'Aṣr** (Late Afternoon Prayer) — صَلَاةُ الْعَصْرِ

4 **Ṣalātul Maghrib** (After Sunset Prayer) — صَلَاةُ الْمَغْرِبِ

5 **Ṣalātul 'Ishā'** (Night Prayer) — صَلَاةُ الْعِشَاءِ

Timings of Aṣ-Ṣalāh

Aṣ-Ṣalāh must be offered at fixed times. Allāh says in the *Qur'ān : "Ṣalāh at set times has been made a duty on the believers."* (Sūratun Nisā' 4 : 103) The timings of *Aṣ-Ṣalāh* are :

1	**Fajr**	*From dawn until just before sunrise*
2	**Ẓuhr**	*After mid-day until afternoon*
3	**'Aṣr**	*From late afternoon until just before sunset*
4	**Maghrib**	*After sunset until daylight ends*
5	**'Ishā'**	*Night until mid-night or dawn*

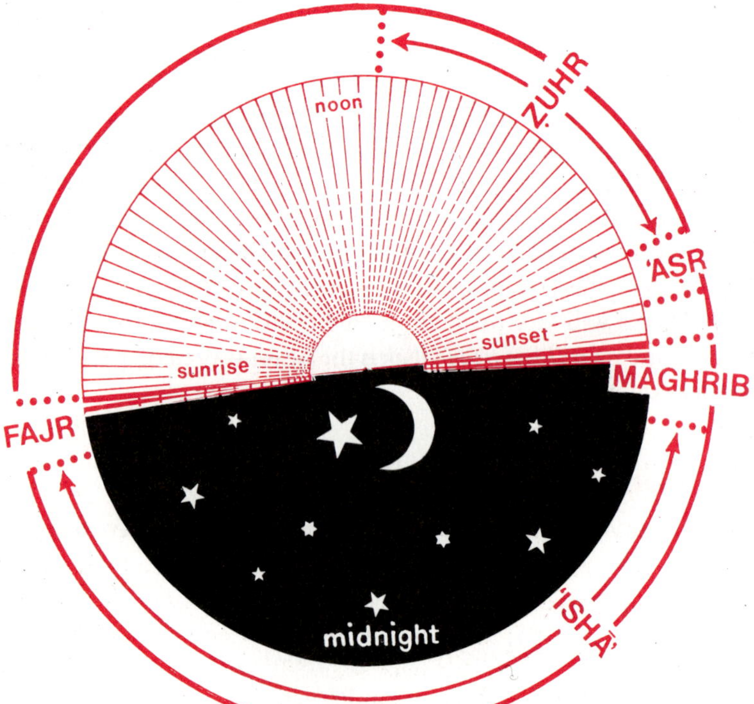

Timings of five daily Ṣalāh

Preparation for Aṣ-Ṣalāh 2

Ṭahārah اَلطَّهَارَة

Aṣ-Ṣalāh has to be performed as Allāh commanded and as shown by Prophet *Muḥammad* (Pbuh). It has to be offered in a particular way. It needs some preparation. This preparation involves *Ṭahārah*. *Ṭahārah* means to be clean and pure. Allāh says in the *Qur'ān* : *"Surely Allāh loves those who turn to Him and those who care for cleanliness."* (Sūratul Baqarah 2 : 222) Prophet *Muḥammad* said : "(i) Purification is the key to Aṣ-Ṣalāh. (ii) Religion is built on cleanliness. (iii) Purification is one-half of faith."

How can we have *Ṭahārah?* To have *Ṭahārah* for our body, we can have *Ghusl* (Full wash) with clean water and we can have *Wuḍū'* (Ablution) which has to be done in a particular way.

Cleanliness of clothes also includes making sure that you do not have any traces of human or animal excrement (e.g. urine, stool) on your clothes. Islām emphasises physical cleanliness as well as the cleanliness of the heart. Cleanliness of the heart means making sure that it is free from the idea of false gods; only the Creator — Allāh — is to be worshipped.

There are certain circumstances when you must have *Ghusl* اَلْغُسْل (Full wash of the body) with clean water. Under these circumstances only *Wuḍū'* اَلْوُضُوْء is not enough for saying *Aṣ-Ṣalāh*. They are :

1 After sexual intercourse between husband and wife.
2 After discharge or ejaculation of semen.
3 For women, after menstruation and up to 40 days after childbirth.

The compulsory (Farḍ) aspects of *Ghusl* are : (i) Rinsing the mouth thoroughly, (ii) Rinsing the nose up to the nasal bone, (iii) Washing all the parts of the body (including the hair) thoroughly. The steps to take for *Ghusl* are : Make Niyyah (Intention) that you are having *Ghusl* to purify yourself from impurity; wash your hands up to the wrists three times and then wash your private parts thoroughly; make *Wuḍū'* and, finally, pour water on all parts of the body, including your hair, and wash your whole body three times.

Conditions for Aṣ-Ṣalāh

1 Cleanliness of the whole body.
2 Cleanliness of clothes.

3 Cleanliness of the place of prayer.

4 For males, covering of the body from the navel to the knees. For females, covering the whole body except the face, feet below the ankles and the hands.

5 Facing *Al-Ka'bah* (Qiblah).

6 Making *Niyyah* (Intention).

7 Offering *Aṣ-Ṣalāh* at set times.

8 Saying *Aṣ-Ṣalāh* in Arabic.

Wuḍū' اَلْوُضُوْءُ

Before we begin to say *Aṣ-Ṣalāh*, we must first prepare ourselves. We must make sure that our body, clothes and the place of *Aṣ-Ṣalāh* are clean. Cleansing parts of the body for the purpose of *Aṣ-Ṣalāh* is called *Wuḍū'*.

Allāh says in the *Qur'ān* : *"Oh you who believe, when you prepare for Aṣ-Ṣalāh, wash your faces and your hands to the elbows; rub your heads and wash your feet up to the ankles. And if you are unclean, purify yourself."* (Sūratul Mā'idah 5 : 6)

This verse clearly points out the compulsory aspects of *Wuḍū'*. These are : (i) washing the face, (ii) washing the hands up to the elbows, (iii) wiping the head with wet palms, (iv) washing the feet up to the ankles. There are also the *Sunnah* (practices) of Prophet *Muḥammad* (Pbuh).

Wuḍū' is essential for performing *Aṣ-Ṣalāh*. We cannot offer *Aṣ-Ṣalāh* without first making *Wuḍū'*. The steps to take for *Wuḍū'* are :

a Make *Niyyah* (intention) saying *Bismillāhir raḥmānir raḥīm*[1] (In the name of Allāh, the most Merciful, the most Kind); then wash both hands up to the wrists three times making sure that water has reached between the fingers.

[1] بِسْمِ اللهِ الرَّحْمٰنِ الرَّحِيْمِ

b Put a handful of water into the mouth and rinse it thoroughly three times.

c Sniff water into the nostrils three times to clean them and then wash the tip of the nose.

d Wash the face three times from right ear to left ear and from forehead to throat.

e Wash the right arm, and then left arm, thoroughly from wrist to elbow three times.

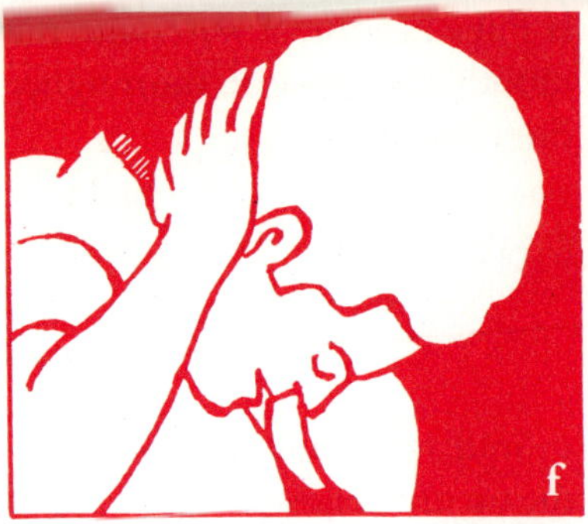

f Move the wet palms of both hands over the head, starting from the top of the forehead to the neck.

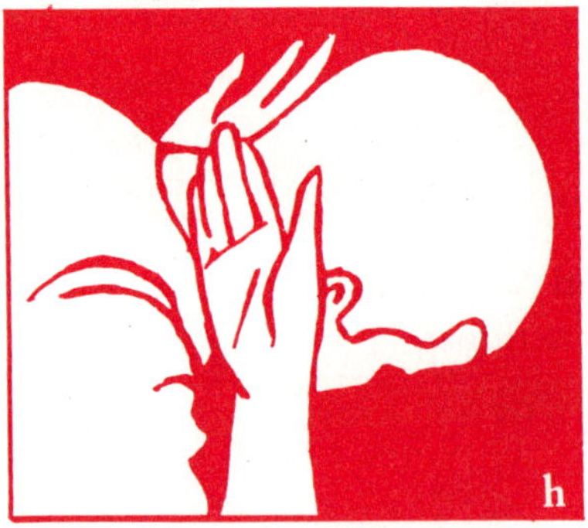

g Rub the wet fingers into the grooves and holes of both ears and also pass the wet thumbs behind the ears.

h Pass the backs of the wet hands over the nape.

i Wash both feet to the ankles starting from the right foot and making sure that water has reached between the toes and all other parts of the feet.

If you made a complete *Wuḍū'* before putting on your socks, it is not necessary to take them off every time you repeat your *Wuḍū'*; it is enough to wipe the upper part of the socks with wet fingers. Leather socks are preferred for this, but any durable, untorn thick socks can serve the purpose. This type of wiping is valid for twenty-four hours only (three days in the case of a journey).

At the end of all the steps, recite :

أَشْهَدُ أَنْ لَّآ إِلٰهَ إِلَّا اللّٰهُ وَحْدَهٗ لَا شَرِيْكَ لَهٗ
وَأَشْهَدُ أَنَّ مُحَمَّدًا عَبْدُهٗ وَرَسُوْلُهٗ

Ash hadu al lā ilāha illal lāhu waḥdahu lā sharīkalahu wa ash hadu anna muḥammadan 'abduhu wa rasūluhu.

I testify that there is no god but Allāh and He is one and has no partner and I also testify that *Muḥammad* is His servant and messenger.

You should repeat your Wuḍū' after :

1 *Natural discharges (e.g. urine, stool, wind and the like).*
2 *Flow of blood or pus from any part of the body.*
3 *Full mouth vomiting.*
4 *Falling asleep.*

Tayammum (Dry Ablution) اَلتَّيَمُّمُ

Islām is a very practical way of life. It has not laid down any impossible duties for us. For instance, if you cannot make *Wuḍū'* for any of the following reasons :

1 *water is not available at all,*
2 *the water available is insufficient (e.g. available water is enough for drinking only), or*
3 *use of water is harmful (e.g. in sickness)*

then you are allowed to make *Tayammum* and offer your *Ṣalāh*.

For *Tayammum* you are required to :

1 Make *Niyyah* by saying : *Bismillāhir raḥmānir raḥīm* and place both your hands lightly on earth, sand, stone or any other object having dust on it.

2 Blow the dust off your hands and wipe your face with the hands once the same way as you do in *Wuḍū'*

3 Repeat 1 and wipe the right arm from wrist to the elbow with the left hand and the left arm with the right hand.

Adhān (Call to Prayer) اَلْاَذَان

Farḍ (Compulsory) *Ṣalāh* should preferably be offered in the mosque in congregation. All other *Ṣalāh* can be offered privately at home. To call Muslims to *Ṣalāh*, Prophet *Muḥammad* (Pbuh) introduced the system of *Adhān*. *Adhān* signals that the time of *Ṣalāh* has arrived.

The person who gives *Adhān* is called the *Mu'adhdhin* (Caller). Allāh says in the *Qur'ān*, *"Who speaks better than one who calls to Allāh and acts righteously."* (Surah Ḥāmīm As-Sajdah 41 : 33)

The first *Mu'adhdhin* of Islām in *Madīnah* was *Bilāl Ibn Rabāḥ*. When calling the *Adhān*, the *Mu'adhdhin* stands in the minaret or in the courtyard of the mosque, faces the *Qiblah*, raises his hands to his ears and calls out :

اَللهُ اَكْبَرُ ط	اَللهُ اَكْبَرُ ط	اَللهُ اَكْبَرُ ط	اَللهُ اَكْبَرُ ط
Allāhu Akbar	*Allāhu Akbar*	*Allāhu Akbar*	*Allāhu Akbar*
(Allāh is the Greatest)	(Allāh is the Greatest)	(Allāh is the Greatest)	(Allāh is the Greatest

اَشْهَدُ اَنْ لَّا اِلٰهَ اِلَّا اللهُ ط	اَشْهَدُ اَنْ لَّا اِلٰهَ اِلَّا اللهُ ط
Ashhadu al lā ilāha illallāh	*Ashhadu al lā ilāha illalāh*
(I testify that there is no god but Allāh)	(I testify that there is no god but Allāh)

أَشْهَدُ أَنَّ مُحَمَّدًا رَّسُولُ اللهِ ط

Ashhadu anna muḥammadar rasūlullāh

(I testify that Muḥammad is Allāh's messenger)

أَشْهَدُ أَنَّ مُحَمَّدًا رَّسُولُ اللهِ ط

Ashhadu anna muḥammadar rasūlullāh

(I testify that Muḥammad is Allāh's messenger)

حَيَّ عَلَى الصَّلٰوةِ ط

Ḥayya 'alaṣ ṣalāh

(Rush to Ṣalāh)

حَيَّ عَلَى الصَّلٰوةِ ط

Ḥayya 'alaṣ ṣalāh

(Rush to Ṣalāh)

حَيَّ عَلَى الْفَلَاحِ ط

Ḥayya 'alal falāḥ

(Rush to success)

حَيَّ عَلَى الْفَلَاحِ ط

Ḥayya 'alal falāḥ

(Rush to success)

اَللهُ أَكْبَرُ ط

Allāhu Akbar

(Allāh is the Greatest)

اَللهُ أَكْبَرُ ط

Allāhu Akbar

(Allāh is the Greatest)

لَآ إِلٰهَ إِلَّا اللهُ ط

Lā ilāha illal lāh

(There is no god but Allāh)

During the *Adhān* for *Fajr Ṣalāh* the following words are added after *Ḥayya 'alal falāḥ* :

اَلصَّلٰوةُ خَيْرٌ مِّنَ النَّوْمِ ط

Aṣṣalātu khairum minan nawm

(Ṣalāh is better than sleep)

اَلصَّلٰوةُ خَيْرٌ مِّنَ النَّوْمِ ط

Aṣṣalātu khairum minan nawm

(Ṣalāh is better than sleep)

Iqāmah اَلْإِقَامَة

Iqāmah is the second call to *Ṣalāh* said inside the mosque at the beginning of *Ṣalāh* in congregation *(Jama'ah)*. When the *muṣallis* (persons saying Ṣalāh) stand in rows, the *Mu'adhdhin* says *Iqāmah* which is the same as the *Adhān* except that after *Ḥayya 'alal falāḥ*, the following words are added :

قَدْ قَامَتِ الصَّلٰوةُ ط

Qad Qāmatiṣ Ṣalāh
(Ṣalāh has begun)

قَدْ قَامَتِ الصَّلٰوةُ ط

Qad Qāmatiṣ Ṣalāh
(Ṣalāh has begun)

We should repeat the words the *Mu'adhdhin* calls out after him and when he says *Ḥayya 'alaṣ Ṣalāh* and *Ḥayya 'alal falāḥ*, we should say *Lā ḥawlā wala quwwata illa billah* (There is no power and strength except Allāh). After hearing the *Mu'adhdhin* say *Aṣṣalātu khairum minan Nawm*, we should say '— *Sadaqta wa bararta*[1] (You told the truth and you did good). When the *Mu'adhdhin* says, *Qad qāmatiṣ Ṣalāh*, we should say — *Aqāmahāllāhu wa adāmahā*[2] (May Allāh establish it and make it permanent).

Du'ā' after Adhān :- اَلدُّعَاءُ بَعْدَ الْاَذَانِ

اَللّٰهُمَّ رَبَّ هٰذِهِ الدَّعْوَةِ التَّامَّةِ وَالصَّلَاةِ الْقَائِمَةِ اٰتِ مُحَمَّدَ
نِالْوَسِيْلَةَ وَالْفَضِيْلَةَ وَالدَّرَجَةَ الرَّفِيْعَةَ وَابْعَثْهُ مَقَامًا مَّحْمُوْدَ
نِالَّذِيْ وَعَدْتَّهٗ وَارْزُقْنَا شَفَاعَتَهٗ يَوْمَ الْقِيَامَةِ اِنَّكَ لَا تُخْلِفُ
الْمِيْعَادَ ط

Allāhumma rabba hādhihid da'watit tāmmah, wassala til Qā'imah, āti Muḥammadanil wasīlata wal faḍīlata wad darajatar rafī'ah, wab'athhu maqāmum maḥmudanilladhi wa'ad tahu wa arzuqnā shafā'atahu yawmal qiāmah, innaka lā tukhliful mī'ād.

O Allāh, Lord of this complete call and prayer of ours, grant Muḥammad the right of intercession, the most favoured and excellent position and raise him to the praiseworthy place that You have promised him and bestow upon us his intercession on the day of judgement, for You do not fail in your promise.

---

[1] صَدَقْتَ وَبَرَرْتَ   [2] اَقَامَهَا اللّٰهُ وَاَدَامَهَا

3

Details of Aṣ-Ṣalāh

Kinds of Aṣ-Ṣalāh

1 Farḍ اَلْفَرْض These are the compulsory *Ṣalāh* which a Muslim must perform. There are two types of *Farḍ* : *(i) Farḍ 'Ain* فَرْضُ عَيْن These *Ṣalāh* must be performed by every Muslim, e.g. the five daily *Ṣalāh*; (ii) *Farḍ Kifāyah* فَرْضُ كِفَايَة These *Ṣalāh* may not be performed by every Muslim; if some members of the community say them, others will be excused from saying them, e.g. *Ṣalātul Janāzah*.

2 Wājib اَلْوَاجِب These are *Ṣalāh* which also have to be performed and they come next in importance to *Farḍ*, e.g. *Ṣalātul 'Īd* and *Ṣalātul Witr*.

3 Sunnah اَلسُّنَّة These are *Ṣalāh* which Prophet *Muḥammad* (Pbuh) himself said or approved of. There are two types of *Sunnah Ṣalāh* : (i) *Sunnah Mu'akkadah* سُنَّة مُؤَكَّدَة the *Ṣalāh* which the Prophet (Pbuh) always performed without break and (ii) *Sunnah Ghair Mu'akkadah* سُنَّة غَيْر مُؤَكَّدَة These are the *Ṣalāh* which he occasionally performed.

4 Nafl اَلنَّفْل These are *Ṣalāh* which you can say on your own initiative for more reward.

Essentials of Aṣ-Ṣalāh فَرَائِضُ الصَّلَاة

The following are the things which are *Farḍ* or compulsory in *Ṣalāh*.

1 Niyyah اَلنِّيَّة Making the intention for Ṣalāh.

2 Takbīratul Iḥrām تَكْبِيْرَةُ الإِحْرَام Saying *Allāhu Akbar* at the beginning of the *Ṣalāh*.

3 Qiyām اَلْقِيَام Standing upright.

4 Qirā'h اَلْقِرَاءَة Recitation of *Sūratul Fātiḥah* and some verses from the *Qur'ān*.

5 Rukū' اَلرُّكُوع Bowing down in a way so as to form a right angle with legs.

6 Sujūd اَلسُّجُوْد Prostrating in such a way that the palms of both hands, the forehead, the tip of the nose, the knees and the toes of both feet touch the ground; there must be enough space between the arms and the chest and the legs and the belly so that they do not touch each other but remain apart.

7 Al-Qu'ūdul Ākhir اَلْقُعُوْدُ الْاَخِيْر Sitting down in such a way as to keep the right foot upright on the toes and the left foot in a reclining position under the buttocks. This is done at the end of a particular *Ṣalāh*. If it is a two *rak'ah Ṣalāh* it is after the second *rak'ah* and if it is a four *rak'ah Ṣalāh* it is after the fourth *rak'ah*.

8 Salām اَلسَّلَام Turning the head to the right saying *Assalāmu 'Alaikum wa raḥmatullāh* and then to the left repeating *Assalāmu 'Alaikum wa raḥmatullah*. This signifies the completion of *Ṣalāh*.

Wājibātuṣ Ṣalāh وَاجِبَاتُ الصَّلَاة

The following are the fifteen things which should be done in your *Ṣalāh*. They are called *Wājibātuṣ Ṣalāh*. They are next in importance to the eight *Farā'iḍ* mentioned before.

1 To recite *Sūratul Fātiḥah* and some other verses from the *Qur'ān* in the first two *raka'hs* of any *Farḍ Ṣalāh*.

2 To recite *Sūratul Fātiḥah* in every *rak'ah* of every *Ṣalāh*.

3 To recite a small *Sūrah*, a long verse or three small verses in each *rak'ah* of *Ṣalāh* except the third and fourth *rak'ah* of *Farḍ Ṣalāh*.

4 To recite *Sūratul Fātiḥah* before the other Sūrah or verses of the *Qur'ān*.

5 To maintain the order and sequence in the performance of *qiyām, qirā'h, rukū', sujūd, qu'ūd* and *salām*.

6 To stand upright after *rukū'*.

7 To sit up between two *sujūd*.

8 To perform each part of *Ṣalāh* calmly without haste (I'tidal).

9 To sit for reciting the first *Tashahhud* in a three and four *rak'ah Ṣalāh*.

10 To recite *Tashahhud* in both sittings in three and four *rak'ah Ṣalāh*.

11 To recite *Sūratul Fātiḥah* and another Sūrah or verses loudly in the first two *Farḍ rak'ah* of *Fajr, Maghrib, 'Ishā', Jumu'ah* and *Ṣalātul 'Īd* and in all the *raka'hs* of *Tarāwīḥ* and *Witr* during *Ramaḍān*.

12 To finish *Ṣalāh* by saying the words of *Salām*.

13 To recite *Du'ā' Al-Qunūt* in the third *rak'ah* of Witr Ṣalāh.

14 To say six or twelve *Takbīr* in both *'Īd Ṣalāh*.

15 To do *Sajdatus Sahw* in case of mistakes during *Ṣalāh*.

Sunnah of Aṣ-Ṣalāh سُنَنُ الصَّلَاةِ

The following are the Sunnah in *Ṣalāh* :

1 Raising both hands to the ears when saying *Allāhu Akbar*.

2 Facing straight towards the Qiblah when saying *Allāhu Akbar*.

3 The saying aloud by the *Imām* (one who leads *Ṣalāh*) *Allāhu Akbar* in different stages of *Ṣalāh* and *Sami' Allāhuliman Ḥamidah* (Allāh listens to those who praise Him) after *rukū'* at the time of getting up.

4 Placing the right hand over the left hand and below the navel or on the chest.

5 Reciting *Thanā', Ta'awwudh* and *Tasmiyah* silently.

6 Reciting only *Sūratul Fātiḥah* (silently) in the third and fourth *rak'ah* of all *Farḍ Ṣalāh*.

7 Saying *Āmīn* on completing *Sūratul Fātiḥah*.

8 Saying *Subḥana Rabbīal 'Aẓīm* three times in *rukū'* and *Subḥana Rabbīal A'lā* three times in *Sujūd*.

9 Keeping the neck and head straight in *rukū'*.

10 The *Imām* saying *Sami' Allāhu liman Ḥamidah* and the followers (Muqtadis) saying *Rabbana Lakal Ḥamd* (O our Lord, praise be to You).

11 Whilst going into *Sujūd*, the knees have to be placed on the floor first followed by the hands, nose and forehead.

12 Placing palms on thighs when sitting between *sujūd*.

13 Sitting correctly in-between two *sujūd* e.g. placing the feet correctly.

14 Lifting the forefinger of the right hand at the words *Ash hadu anlā ilāha* when reciting *Tashahhud*.

15 Reciting *Aṣ-Ṣalāh 'alan Nabiyy* (Darūd) after the final *Tashahhud*.

16 Turning the head to the right and then to the left in *Salām*.

Farḍ Rak'ah of Aṣ-Ṣalāh

The *Farḍ* (Compulsory) rak'ah of *Aṣ-Ṣalāh* are :

Fajr	....	*2 rak'ah*	
Ẓuhr	....	*4 rak'ah*	
'Aṣr	....	*4 rak'ah*	
Maghrib	....	*3 rak'ah*	
'Ishā'	....	*4 rak'ah*	
		17 rak'ah	
Jumu'ah	....	*2 rak'ah*	*(In place of Ẓuhr on Friday)*

Chart of Aṣ-Ṣalāh

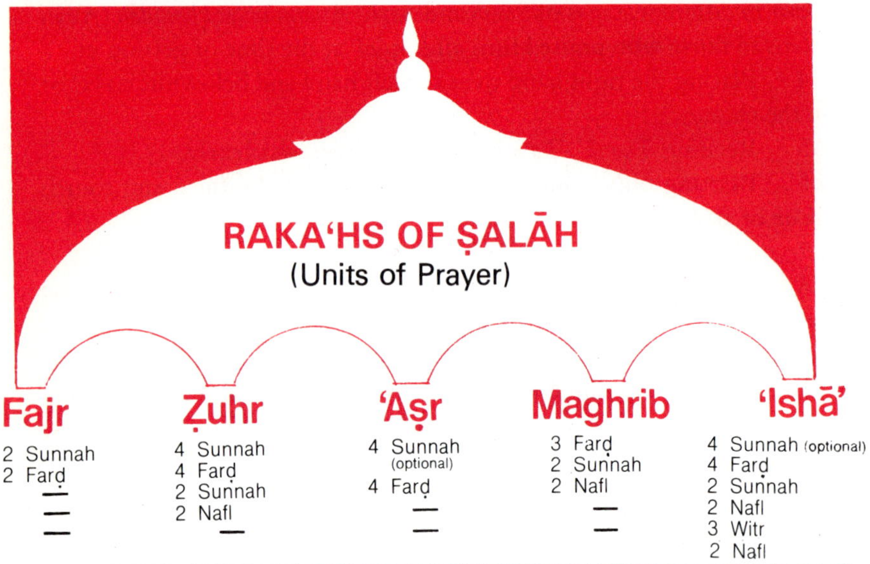

In addition to the five daily *Ṣalāh*, there are occasional *Ṣalāh* e.g. *Ṣalātul Jumu'ah* every Friday, *Ṣalātul 'Īdul Fiṭr, Ṣalātul 'Īdul Aḍḥā* and *Ṣalātul Tarāwīḥ* in the month of Ramaḍān. The raka'hs of these *Ṣalāh* are :

Jumu'ah	'Īdul Fiṭr	'Īdul Aḍḥā	Tarawīḥ
4 Sunnah 2 Farḍ 4 Sunnah 2 Sunnah 2 Nafl	2 Wājib	2 Wājib	20 Sunnah
14	2	2	20

Tarāwīḥ is offered after the two Sunnah *rak'ah* of *'Ishā'* but before the three of *Witr*.

After midnight and before dawn a prayer called *Tahajjud* was regularly offered by Prophet *Muḥammad* (Pbuh). It was obligatory for the Prophet and devout Muslims try to follow the practice.

Times when you must not pray :

1 From the beginning of sunrise until 15-20 minutes after full sunrise.

2 When the sun is at its height (Zenith or Meridian).

3 From the beginning of sunset until it is fully set.

4 For women during menstruation and for up to 40 days after childbirth.

One should not say Nafl Ṣalāh :

1 Between the *Farḍ* of *Ṣalātul Fajr* and sunrise.

2 Between the *Farḍ* of *Ṣalātul 'Aṣr* and sunset.

3 Before the *Farḍ* of *Ṣalātul Maghrib*.

4 During the *Khuṭbahs* of *Ṣalātul Jumu'ah* and *Ṣalātul 'Īd*.

5 Between *Ṣalātul Fajr* and *Ṣalātul 'Īd*.

6 After *Ṣalātul 'Īd* at the place where the *Ṣalāh* has been offered.

7 During *Ḥajj* at *Arafāt* after *Ṣalātul Ẓuhr* and *Ṣalātul 'Aṣr* have been offered together.

8 Between *Ṣalātul Maghrib* and *Ṣalātul 'Ishā'* at *Muzdalifah* during *Ḥajj*.

9 When only a little time is left for saying the *Farḍ* of any *Ṣalāh*.

How to perform Aṣ-Ṣalāh 4

At this stage, you should be ready to actually start saying your *Ṣalāh*. Make sure you have *Wuḍū'*, a clean body, a clean place and clean clothes. The way to offer *Ṣalāh* is :

1 Stand upright on your prayer mat facing the direction of *Al-Ka'bah*. This standing is called *Qiyām* and the direction is called *Qiblah* in Arabic. *Qiblah* is towards the South East in England.

2 Say your *Niyyah* (intention) either verbally or in your mind. Niyyah is said with the words :

	two farḍ**		*Fajr**	
"I intend to say	*three sunnah*	*raka'hs*	*Ẓuhr*	
	four	of Ṣalātul	*'Aṣr*	for Allāh facing *Al-Ka'bah*"
			Maghrib	
			'Ishā'	

3 Raise your hands up to your ears (women and girls up to their shoulders) and say *Allāhu Akbar*[1] (Allāh is the Greatest). This is called *Takbīratul Iḥrām*.

*Say the one which is relevant

1 اللهُ اَكْبَرُ

4 Place your right hand on your left hand just below the navel or on the chest (women and girls put their hands on chest) and recite :

سُبْحَانَكَ اللّٰهُمَّ وَبِحَمْدِكَ وَتَبَارَكَ اسْمُكَ وَتَعَالٰى جَدُّكَ وَلَآ اِلٰهَ غَيْرُكَ

Subḥānaka allāhumma wa bi· ḥamdika wa tabāra kasmuka wa ta'ālā jadduka wa lā ilāha ghairuka.

O Allāh, glory and praise are for You, and blessed is Your name, and exalted is Your Majesty; there is no god but You.

اَعُوْذُ بِاللّٰهِ مِنَ الشَّيْطٰنِ الرَّجِيْمِ ○

A'ūdhu billāhi minash shaiṭānir rajīm

I seek shelter in Allāh from the rejected satan.

بِسْمِ اللّٰهِ الرَّحْمٰنِ الرَّحِيْمِ ○

Bismillāhir raḥmānir raḥīm

In the name of Allāh, the most Merciful, the most Kind.

5 Recite *sūrat-ul-Fātiḥah* (opening chapter) of the *Qur'ān :*

سُوْرَةُ الْفَاتِحَةِ

بِسْمِ اللّٰهِ الرَّحْمٰنِ الرَّحِيْمِ ○

اَلْحَمْدُ لِلّٰهِ رَبِّ الْعٰلَمِيْنَ ○ الرَّحْمٰنِ الرَّحِيْمِ ○ مٰلِكِ يَوْمِ الدِّيْنِ ○
اِيَّاكَ نَعْبُدُ وَاِيَّاكَ نَسْتَعِيْنُ ○ اِهْدِنَا الصِّرَاطَ الْمُسْتَقِيْمَ ○
صِرَاطَ الَّذِيْنَ اَنْعَمْتَ عَلَيْهِمْ ○ غَيْرِ الْمَغْضُوْبِ عَلَيْهِمْ
وَلَا الضَّآلِّيْنَ ○

Al ḥamdu lil lāhi rabbil 'ālamīn. Arraḥmānir raḥīm. Māliki Yawmiddīn. Iyyāka na'budu wa iyyāka nasta'īn. Ihdinaṣ ṣirātal mustaqīm. Ṣirātal ladhīna an 'amta 'alaihim, ghairil maghḍūbi 'alaihim wa laḍ ḍāllīn. (Āmīn).

"All praise is for Allāh, the Lord of the Universe, the most Merciful, the most Kind; Master of the day of judgement. You alone we worship, from You alone we seek help. Guide us along the straight way — the way of those whom You have favoured, not of those who earn Your anger nor of those who go astray."

The recitation of Al-Fātiḥah is a must in all prayers.

6 Recite any other passage from the *Qur'ān*. For example :

بِسْمِ اللهِ الرَّحْمٰنِ الرَّحِيْمِ

Bismillāhir raḥmanir raḥīm

قُلْ هُوَ اللهُ اَحَدٌ ۚ اَللهُ الصَّمَدُ ۚ لَمْ يَلِدْ ۙ وَلَمْ يُوْلَدْ ۙ
وَلَمْ يَكُنْ لَّهٗ كُفُوًا اَحَدٌ

Qul hu wal lāhu aḥad, allāhuṣ ṣamad, lam yalid wa lam yūlud, wa lam ya kul lahu kufuwan aḥad.

In the name of Allāh, the most Merciful, the most Kind.
"Say, He is Allāh, the One. Allāh is Eternal and Absolute. None is born of Him nor is He born and there is none like Him." (Sūratul Ikhlaṣ)

7 Bow down saying : *Allāhu Akbar*[2]. Place your hands on your knees and say : *Subḥāna Rabbīal 'Aẓim*[3] (Glory to my Lord, the Great) three times. This position is called *Rukū'*.

8 Stand up from *Rukū'* saying : *Sami' Allāhu Liman Ḥamidah*[4] (Allāh hears those who praise Him) and *Rabbanā Lakal Ḥamd* (Our Lord, praise be to You). This standing is called *Qiyām*.

2 اللهُ أَكْبَرُ
3 سُبْحَانَ رَبِّيَ الْعَظِيْمِ
4 سَمِعَ اللهُ لِمَنْ حَمِدَهٗ
5 رَبَّنَا لَكَ الْحَمْدُ

9 Prostrate on your prayer mat saying *Allāhu Akbar*[6], with your forehead, nose, palms of both hands and your knees touching the floor. Recite *Subḥāna Rabbīal A'lā*[7] (Glory to my Lord, the Highest) three times. This position is called *Sujūd*. Your arms should not touch the floor.

10 Get up from the floor saying *Allāhu Akbar*[8] and sit upright with your knees bent and palms placed on them. After a moment's rest★ prostrate again on the floor saying : *Allāhu Akbar*[9] and recite *Subḥāna Rabbīal A'lā*[10] three times. Get up from this position saying *Allāhu Akbar*[11].

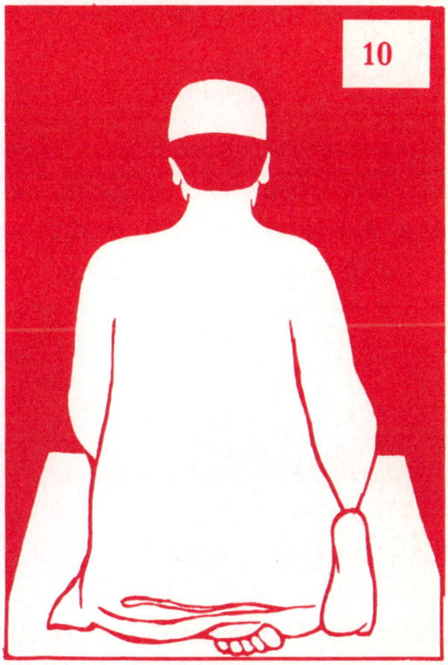

11 اللهُ أكبر　10 سُبحانَ رَبِّيَ الأعلى　9 اللهُ أكبر　8 اللهُ أكبر　7 سُبحانَ رَبِّيَ الأعلى　6 اللهُ أكبر

★Here you can say the Du'ā' : Rabbighfirlī warḥamnī wahdini wa'āfinī warzuqnī

This completes one rak'ah or one unit of *Ṣalāh*. The second rak'ah is performed in the same way, except that you do not recite *Subḥanaka Ta'awwudh* and *Tasmiyah* and after the second prostration you sit upright and recite quietly *At-Tashahhud* :

اَلتَّحِيَّاتُ لِلّٰهِ وَالصَّلَوٰةُ وَالطَّيِّبَاتُ اَلسَّلَامُ عَلَيْكَ اَيُّهَا النَّبِيُّ

وَرَحْمَةُ اللهِ وَبَرَكَاتُهٗ۔ اَلسَّلَامُ عَلَيْنَا وَعَلٰى عِبَادِ اللهِ الصّٰلِحِيْنَ ○

اَشْهَدُ اَنْ لَّآ اِلٰهَ اِلَّا اللهُ وَاَشْهَدُ اَنَّ مُحَمَّدًا عَبْدُهٗ وَرَسُوْلُهٗ ○

At-Taḥiyyātu Lillāhi	— *All prayer is for Allāh*
Waṣ Ṣalawātu Waṭ Ṭayyībātu	— *and worship and goodness*
As-Salāmu 'Alaika Ayyuhannabīyyu	— *Peace be on you, O Prophet*
Wa Raḥmatullāhi Wa Barakātuhu	— *and the mercy of Allāh and His blessings*
Assālamu 'Alainā	— *Peace be on us*
Wa 'Alā 'Ibadillahiṣ Ṣāliḥīn	— *and on the righteous servants of Allāh*
Ash Hādu Al Lāilāha Illal Lāhu	— *I bear witness that there is no god but Allāh*
Wa Ash Hādu Anna Muḥammadan 'Abduhu Wa Rasūluhu	— *and bear witness that Muḥammad is His servant and messenger*

In a three rak'ah *ṣalāh* (as in *Maghrib*) or a four rak'ah *ṣalāh (Ẓuhr, 'Aṣr* and *'Īshā')* you stand up for the remaining rak'ah after *Tashahhud*. But for a two *rak'ah ṣalāh* you remain seated after the second *rak'ah* and recite *Aṣ-Ṣalāh 'alan nabiyy* (blessings for the Prophet) or *Darūd* :

اَللّٰهُمَّ صَلِّ عَلٰى مُحَمَّدٍ وَّعَلٰٓى اٰلِ مُحَمَّدٍ كَمَا صَلَّيْتَ عَلٰٓى اِبْرٰهِيْمَ

وَعَلٰٓى اٰلِ اِبْرٰهِيْمَ اِنَّكَ حَمِيْدٌ مَّجِيْدٌ ○

Allāhumma Ṣalli 'Alā Muḥammadin	— *O Allāh, let Your blessings come upon Muḥammad*
Wa 'Alā Āli Muḥammadin	— *and the family of Muḥammad*
Kamā Ṣallaita 'Alā Ibrāhīma Wa 'Alā Āli Ibrāhīma	— *as You blessed Ibrāhīm and his family*
Innaka Ḥamīdum Majīd	— *truly You are the Praiseworthy and Glorious*

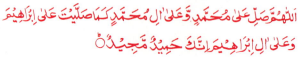

اَللّٰهُمَّ بَارِكْ عَلٰى مُحَمَّدٍ وَّعَلٰى اٰلِ مُحَمَّدٍ كَمَا بَارَكْتَ عَلٰى
إِبْرَاهِيْمَ وَعَلٰى اٰلِ إِبْرَاهِيْمَ إِنَّكَ حَمِيْدٌ مَّجِيْدٌ ۝

Allāhumma Bārik 'Alā Muḥammadin Wa 'Alā Āli Muḥammadin	— *O Allāh, bless Muḥammad and the family of Muḥammad*
Kamā Bārakta 'Alā Ibrāhīma Wa 'Alā Ali Ibrāhīma	— *as You blessed Ibrāhīm and his family*
Innaka Ḥamīdum Majīd	— *truly You are the Praiseworthy and Glorious.*

After this, say any of the following *Du'ā'* (supplication) :

اَللّٰهُمَّ إِنِّيْ ظَلَمْتُ نَفْسِيْ ظُلْمًا كَثِيْرًا وَّلَا يَغْفِرُ الذُّنُوْبَ إِلَّا أَنْتَ
فَاغْفِرْ لِيْ مَغْفِرَةً مِّنْ عِنْدِكَ وَارْحَمْنِيْ إِنَّكَ أَنْتَ الْغَفُوْرُ الرَّحِيْمُ ۝

Allāhumma innī ẓalamtu nafsī ẓulman kathīran wa lā yaghfirudh dhunūba illā anta faghfirlī maghfiratan min 'indika wa arḥamnī innaka antal ghafūrur raḥīm.

O Allāh, I have been unjust to myself and no-one grants pardon for sins except You, therefore, forgive me with Your forgiveness and have mercy on me. Surely, You are the Forgiver, the Merciful.

رَبِّ اجْعَلْنِيْ مُقِيْمَ الصَّلٰوةِ وَمِنْ ذُرِّيَّتِيْ رَبَّنَا وَتَقَبَّلْ دُعَاءِ ۝
رَبَّنَا اغْفِرْ لِيْ وَلِوَالِدَيَّ وَلِلْمُؤْمِنِيْنَ يَوْمَ يَقُوْمُ الْحِسَابُ -

Rabbij'alnī muqīmas salāti wa min dhurriyyati rabbanā wa taqabbal du'ā'. Rabbanāghfirlī waliwālidaiyya wa lil mu'minīna yawma yaqūmul ḥisāb.

O Lord, make me and my children steadfast in Ṣalāh. Our Lord, accept the prayer. Our Lord forgive me and my parents and the believers on the day of judgment.

11 Now turn your face to the right saying : *Assālmu 'Alaikum Wa Raḥmatullāh*[12] (peace and the mercy of Allāh be upon you) and then to the left repeating the words.

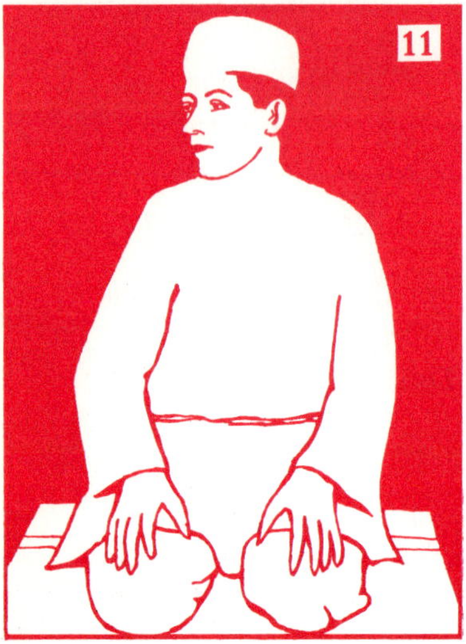

12. اَلسَّلَامُ عَلَيْكُمْ وَرَحْمَةُ اللهِ

This completes the two rak'ah Ṣalāh. In the four rak'ah *Ṣalāh* of *Ẓuhr, 'Aṣr* and *"Īshā'*, the whole procedure is repeated except that when you get up to complete the remaining two rak'ah (one rak'ah in *Maghrib* and *Witr*) after *Tashahhud*, you only recite *Al-Fātiḥah* in Farḍ prayers and no other *surāh*.

In the first two rak'ah of the *Farḍ* prayer of *Fajr, Maghrib* and *'Īshā'* the *Qur'ān* is recited aloud while in *Ẓuhr* and *'Aṣr* it is recited silently. In all prayers, Tasbīḥ *(Subḥāna Rabbīal 'Aẓīm* and *Subḥāna Rabbīal a'lā), Tashahhud* and *Darūd* are said quietly. When the *Fajr, Maghrib* and *'Ishā'* prayers are said in congregation, only the *Imām* (one who leads the prayer) recites the *Qur'ān* aloud. This also applies to *Jumu'ah* prayer *(Friday Prayer in place of Ẓuhr)*.

Salātul Witr صَلَاةُ الْوِتْر :-

The Witr (odd number) prayer has three Raka'hs. The first two Raka'hs are said like the first two Raka'hs of the *Maghrib* prayer then, after *Tashahhud* in the second Rak'ah, stand up saying *Allāhu Akbar* for the third rak'ah. Recite *Sūratul Fātiḥah* and some other verses from the *Qur'ān* but before going to Rukū' raise your hands up to the ears saying *Allāhu Akbar* and recite the following du'ā' after placing your hands below your navel or on the chest. This du'ā is called *Du'ā' al-Qunūt*.

اَللّٰهُمَّ إِنَّا نَسْتَعِينُكَ وَنَسْتَغْفِرُكَ وَنُؤْمِنُ بِكَ وَنَتَوَكَّلُ عَلَيْكَ وَنُثْنِي
عَلَيْكَ الْخَيْرَ وَنَشْكُرُكَ وَلَا نَكْفُرُكَ وَنَخْلَعُ وَنَتْرُكُ مَنْ يَّفْجُرُكَ.
اَللّٰهُمَّ إِيَّاكَ نَعْبُدُ وَلَكَ نُصَلِّي وَنَسْجُدُ وَإِلَيْكَ نَسْعٰى وَنَحْفِدُ
وَنَرْجُوْ رَحْمَتَكَ وَنَخْشٰى عَذَابَكَ إِنَّ عَذَابَكَ بِالْكُفَّارِ مُلْحِقٌ.

Allāhumma innā nasta'īnuka wa nastaghfiruka, wa nu'minu bika wa natawakkalu 'alaika wa nuthnī 'alaikal khair, wa nashkuruka wa lā nakfuruka wa nakhla'u wa natruku manyyafjuruka, allāhumma iyyāka na'budu, wa laka nuṣallī wa nasjudu wa ilaika nas'ā wa naḥfidu wa narjū raḥmataka wa nakhsha 'adhābaka inna 'adhābaka bil kuffāri mulḥiq.

O Allāh, we seek Your help and ask Your forgiveness and we believe in You and trust in You. We praise You in the best way and we thank You and we are not ungrateful and we cast off and forsake him who disobeys You. O Allāh, You alone we worship and to You we pray and before you we prostrate, to You we turn in haste, and hope for Your mercy and fear Your punishment. Your punishment overtakes the unbelievers.

After this, say *Allāhu Akbar* and bow down in rukū' and complete the rest of the prayer like the *Maghrib* prayer.

Sajdatus Sahw (Prostration of forgetfulness) سَجْدَةُ السَّهْوِ :-

Since we are human beings, we are not above mistakes and errors. If we forget to do something in our *ṣalāh*, we can make up for it by making two extra *sujūd* as we do in any rak'ah of ṣalāh. This is called *Sajdatus Sahw*. This is done at the end of the last rak'ah of *ṣalāh*. What you have to do is say Tashahhud and then turn your face to the right, say *Assalāmu 'alaikum wa raḥmatullāh* and make two extra *sujūd* (with tasbīḥ *Subḥāna Rabbīal a'lā*) and then recite *Tashahhud* again with *Aṣ-Ṣalāh 'alan Nabiyy* (Darūd) and du'ā'. Then turn your face, first to the right and then to the left, saying *Assalāmu 'alaikum wa raḥmatullāh*.

Sajdatus Sahw is necessary if you forget to do any essentials of ṣalāh, for example, the recitation of parts of the *Qurān* after *Al-Fātiḥah*, forgetting to say the first *Tashahhud* in a four rak'ah *ṣalāh*, or saying *salām* after two raka'hs in a four rak'ah ṣalāh.

Your ṣalāh will not be valid if you do any of the following :

1 Miss out Niyyah (intention).

2 Miss out Takbīratul Iḥrām.

3 Forget to recite Al-Fātiḥah.

4 Forget or do not make rukū' or sujūd.

5 Do not face Qiblah.

6 Do not have Wuḍū'.

7 Talk during ṣalāh.

8 Eat or drink during ṣalāh.

9 Do not sit for Tashahhud.

Under these circumstances, you must repeat your *ṣalāh*. *Sajdatus Sahw* will not be enough.

Some Du'ā' After Prayer بَعْضُ الْأَدْعِيَةِ بَعْدَ الصَّلَاةِ

It is good practice to ask for forgiveness and mercy from Allāh at the end of your *ṣalāh*. You can say this in your own words and in your own language but it is better for you to memorise some du'ā' in Arabic.

رَبَّنَآ اٰتِنَا فِي الدُّنْيَا حَسَنَةً وَّفِي الْاٰخِرَةِ حَسَنَةً وَّقِنَا عَذَابَ النَّارِ ○

Rabbanā ātinā fidduniā ḥasanah wa fil ākhirati ḥasanah wa qinā ʻadhābannār.

O Our Lord, grant us good in this world and good in the hereafter and save us from the punishment of Hell-fire.

اَللّٰهُمَّ اَنْتَ السَّلَامُ وَمِنْكَ السَّلَامُ تَبَارَكْتَ يَا ذَا الْجَلَالِ وَالْاِكْرَامِ

Allāhumma antas salāmu wa minkas salāmu tabārakta yā dhāljalāli wal ikrām.

O Allāh, You are the source of peace and from You comes peace, exalted You are, O Lord of Majesty and Honour.

اَللّٰهُمَّ اغْفِرْلِيْ وَلِوَالِدَيَّ وَلِاُسْتَاذِيْ وَلِجَمِيْعِ الْمُؤْمِنِيْنَ وَالْمُؤْمِنَاتِ
وَالْمُسْلِمِيْنَ وَالْمُسْلِمَاتِ بِرَحْمَتِكَ يَآ اَرْحَمَ الرّٰحِمِيْنَ ○

Allāhummaghfirlī waliwālidaiyya waliustādhī wali jamīʻil muʻminīna, walmu'minati wal muslimīna wal muslimāti biraḥmatika yā ʻarḥamurrāhimīn.

O Allāh, forgive me and my parents and my teachers and all the believing men and women and all muslim men and women with Your Mercy. O Most Merciful of all who have mercy.

رَبَّنَا ظَلَمْنَآ اَنْفُسَنَا وَاِنْ لَّمْ تَغْفِرْلَنَا وَتَرْحَمْنَا لَنَكُوْنَنَّ مِنَ الْخٰسِرِيْنَ ○

Rabbanā ẓalamnā anfusanā wa illam taghfirlanā wa tarḥamnā lana kunanna minal khāsirīn.

Our Lord, we have wronged ourselves and if You do not forgive us and have no mercy on us, surely we will be of the losers.

5

Aṣ-Ṣalāh on Special Occasions

Ṣalātul Jumu'ah (Friday Prayer) :- صَلاةُ الْجُمُعَة

Ṣalātul Jumu'ah or Friday Prayer is offered in congregation. All adult Muslim men must take part. It is offered on *Friday* during *Ẓuhr* time. It is not a must for women, but they can join this prayer if it does not upset their household duties.

People assemble for this *Ṣalāh* immediately after noon. On arriving at the mosque or the prayer hall, they offer 4 or more raka'hs *Sunnah* prayer and then the *Imām* (prayer leader) delivers a *Khutbah* (sermon). After the *khutbah*, the *Imām* leads two rak'ah *Farḍ* prayer. After the *Farḍ* prayer, 6 or more raka'hs of *Sunnah* and *Nafl* prayers are offered individually by each person.

Muslims are a community. *Ṣalātul Jumu'ah* is a community prayer. Every week, on *Friday*, Muslims living in an area get together to offer this prayer.

Mosques were the centre of all Islamic activities during our Prophet's time, but this is not so nowadays.

Friday prayer is an occasion for the assembly of Muslims in an area. It gives them the opportunity to meet, discuss and solve their community problems. It develops unity, co-operation and cohesiveness.

In an Islamic state, the Head of State or his representative is supposed to lead the five daily prayers and the *Friday Prayer* at the central mosque of the capital as was done by Prophet *Muḥammad* (Pbuh) — the first head of the Islamic State in *Madīnah*.

How wonderful it would be to live in a country where the Head of State or his representative leads the prayer in the central mosque of the capital! This practice of the Prophet must be revived in all Islamic States.

Ṣalātul Janāzah (Funeral Prayer) :- صَلاةُ الْجَنَازَة

Death is a natural event. It is sure to come in everyone's life. When a Muslim dies, the body is given a wash and then a funeral prayer called

Ṣalātul Janāzah is offered in congregation. This *ṣalāh*, unlike other *ṣalāh*, has neither any *rukū'* (bowing) nor any *sujūd* (prostration) and you don't have to recite *Tashahhud*.

It is a collective obligation *(Farḍ Kifāyah)* on all the Muslims of the locality of the dead person. If a number of them join in the obligation is discharged on behalf of all. If no-one joins in everyone of the locality will be considered sinful before Allāh. This is how the prayer is offered :

1 Make *niyyah* (intention) that you are saying this prayer to Allāh for the dead person.

2 Stand in rows facing Qiblah. The coffin is placed in front of the congregation in a bier.

3 Say *Allāhu Akbar* after the *Imām* (this takbīr is *Takbīratul Iḥrām* and there will be three more takbīrat after this) and raise your hands up to your ears; bring them down again and place them on or below your chest, putting the right hand on the left and recite the following :

سُبْحَانَكَ اللّٰهُمَّ وَبِحَمْدِكَ وَتَبَارَكَ اسْمُكَ وَتَعَالٰى جَدُّكَ
وَجَلَّ ثَنَاؤُكَ وَلَآ اِلٰهَ غَيْرُكَ

Subḥānaka allāhumma wa biḥamdika wa tabārkasmuka wa ta'lā jadduka wa jalla thanāu'ka wa lā ilāha ghairuka.

O Allāh, Glory and Praise are for You and blessed is Your name, and exalted is Your Majesty and Glorious is Your Praise and there is no god but You.

Then the *Imām* will say *'Allāhu Akbar'* loudly and you have to follow him repeating the words quietly. There is no need to raise your hands up to your ears this time. Now, recite the following *Darūd :*

اَللّٰهُمَّ صَلِّ عَلٰى مُحَمَّدٍ وَّعَلٰٓى اٰلِ مُحَمَّدٍ كَمَا صَلَّيْتَ عَلٰٓى اِبْرَاهِيْمَ
وَعَلٰٓى اٰلِ اِبْرَاهِيْمَ اِنَّكَ حَمِيْدٌ مَّجِيْدٌ ۝

Allāhumma ṣalli 'alā Muḥammadin wa 'alā āli Muḥammadin kamā ṣallaita 'alā Ibrāhīma wa 'alā āli Ibrāhīma innaka ḥamīdum majīd.

O Allāh, let Your blessing come upon Muḥammad and the family of Muḥammad as You blessed Ibrāhim and his family. Truly You are the Praiseworthy and Glorious.

اَللّٰهُمَّ بَارِكْ عَلٰى مُحَمَّدٍ وَّعَلٰٓى اٰلِ مُحَمَّدٍ كَمَا بَارَكْتَ عَلٰى
اِبْرَاهِيْمَ وَعَلٰٓى اٰلِ اِبْرَاهِيْمَ اِنَّكَ حَمِيْدٌ مَّجِيْدٌ ○

Allāhumma bārik 'alā Muḥammadin wa 'alā āli Muḥammadin kamā bārakta 'alā Ibrāhim wa 'alā āli Ibrāhīma innaka ḥamīdum majīd.

O Allāh, bless Muḥammad and the family of Muḥammad as You blessed Ibrāhim and his family. Truly You are the Praiseworthy and Glorious.

After this, the second *Takbīr* will be said loudly by the *Imām* and those in the congregation will repeat it quietly. Then, if the dead person is an adult male Muslim, recite the following *Du'ā'* :

اَللّٰهُمَّ اغْفِرْ لِحَيِّنَا وَمَيِّتِنَا وَشَاهِدِنَا وَغَائِبِنَا وَصَغِيْرِنَا
وَكَبِيْرِنَا وَذَكَرِنَا وَاُنْثَانَا ۔ اَللّٰهُمَّ مَنْ اَحْيَيْتَهٗ مِنَّا
فَاَحْيِهٖ عَلَى الْاِسْلَامِ وَمَنْ تَوَفَّيْتَهٗ مِنَّا فَتَوَفَّهٗ عَلَى الْاِيْمَانِ

Allāhummaghfir liḥayyinā wa mayyitinā wa shāhidinā wa ghā'ibinā wa ṣaghirinā wa kabirinā wa dhakarinā wa unthānā allāhumma man aḥyaitahu minnā fāaḥyihi 'alal Islām wa man tawaffaitahu minnā fatawaffahu 'alal īmān.

O Allāh, forgive those of us who are still alive and those who have passed away, those present and those absent and our young and the elderly, the males and the females. O Allāh, the one whom You wish to keep alive from among us make him live according to Islām and anyone whom You wish to die from among us, let him die in the state of *īmān* (faith).

If the dead person is an adult woman, then the second part of this *Du'ā'* is replaced by :

اَللّٰهُمَّ مَنْ اَحْيَيْتَهَا مِنَّا فَاَحْيِهَا عَلَى الْاِسْلَامِ
وَمَنْ تَوَفَّيْتَهَا مِنَّا فَتَوَفَّهَا عَلَى الْاِيْمَانِ

Allāhumma man aḥyaitahā minnā fa aḥyihā 'alāl Islām, wa man tawaffaitahā minnā fatawaffahā 'alāl īmān.

O Allāh, she to whom You wish to keep alive from us, make her live according to Islām and she to whom You wish to die from among us, let her die in the state of īmān.

If the deceased is a boy, then recite the following :

اَللّٰهُمَّ اجْعَلْهُ لَنَا فَرَطًا وَّاجْعَلْهُ لَنَا اَجْرًا وَّذُخْرًا وَّاجْعَلْهُ لَنَا
شَافِعًا وَّمُشَفَّعًا ۔

Allāhummaj'alhu lanā farṭān waj'alhu lanā ajrān wa dhukhrān waj'alhu lanā shāfi'ān wa mushaff'ān.

O Allāh, make him our forerunner and make him for us a reward and a treasure; make him one who will plead for us, and accept his pleading.

If the deceased is a girl, then recite the following :

اَللّٰهُمَّ اجْعَلْهَا لَنَا فَرَطًا وَّاجْعَلْهَا لَنَا اَجْرًا وَّذُخْرًا وَّاجْعَلْهَا
لَنَا شَافِعَةً وَّمُشَفَّعَةً ۔

Allāhummaj'alha lanā farṭān waj'alhā lanā ajrān wa dhukhrān waj'alhā lanā shāfi'atan wa mushaff'āh.

O Allāh, make her our forerunner and make her for us a reward and a treasure; make her one who will plead for us and accept her pleading.

After reciting whichever *du'ā'* accords to the status of the dead person, the *Īmām* says *Allāhu Akbar* loudly and you repeat the words *Allāhu Akbar* quietly.

Then the *Īmām* turns his face first to the right saying *Assalāmu 'alaikum wa Raḥmatullāh* and then to the left repeating the same words. Follow the *Īmām*, repeating the Arabic words quietly.

This completes *Ṣalātul Janāzah.*

Ṣalātul ʻĪdain صَلَاةُ الْعِيدَيْنِ

There are two main festivals of Islām in each year : ʻĪdul Fiṭr and ʻĪdul Aḍḥā. On both occasions a two rakʻah *Ṣalāh* is offered in congregation, normally after sunrise but before noon. No *Adhān* or *Iqāmah* is said. The special point to note is that *Ṣalātul ʻĪd* is said with six or twelve *Takbīr* (Allāhu Akbar). You say three or seven *Takbīr* in the first *rakʻah* after *Thanā'* (Subḥanaka) or *Takbīratul Iḥrām* and three or five *Takbīr* in the second *rakʻah* before you do *rukūʻ*. The rest is exactly like the two *Farḍ* of *Ṣalātul Jumuʻah* except that the *Khutbah* (Sermon) is given after the prayer. You may recall in *Ṣalātul Jumuʻah*, the *Khutbah* is given before the two *Farḍ* rakʻah. All Muslims, including women and children, should join *Ṣalātul ʻĪd*.

Ṣalātul Musāfir صَلَاةُ الْمُسَافِرِ

A Muslim who is on a journey is allowed to shorten a four rakʻah *Farḍ Ṣalāh* to two rakʻah. Two and three rakʻah *Farḍ Ṣalāh* remain as they are. This means that the four rakʻah *Farḍ* of *Ẓuhr*, ʻAṣr and *ʻIshā'* will be shortened to two rakʻah each. The *Farḍ* of *Fajr* and *Farḍ* of *Maghrib* remain unchanged. Allāh says in the *Qur'ān* : *"And when you go forth in the land, it is no sin for you to shorten your Ṣalāh."* (Sūratun Nisā' 4 : 101)

Prophet *Muḥammad* (Pbuh) used to say two rakʻah Sunnah before two rakʻah *Farḍ* at the time of *Fajr* and three rakʻah of *Witr* even when on a journey.

You can shorten *Farḍ Ṣalāh* on a journey if :

i you are forty-eight miles or more away from home

ii you have the intention of staying less than fifteen days in one place during the journey. If after fifteen days, you change your intention and stay a few days more, you can still shorten the four rakʻah *Farḍ* of *Ẓuhr, ʻAṣr* and *ʻIshā'* and leave out all *Sunnah* and *Nafl Ṣalāh*.

A *Musāfir* (Traveller) must follow the *Imām* in *Farḍ Ṣalāh*. In other words if the *Imām* is a local man (Muqīm), the *Musāfir* will say the full four rakʻah *Farḍ Ṣalāh* during *Ẓuhr, ʻAṣr* and *ʻIshā'*. But if the *Imām* is a *Musāfir* himself, then the *Musāfir* follower (Muqtadī) will follow the *Imām* i.e. he will also say a shortened *Ṣalāh* like the *Imām*.

Ṣalātul Istikhārah صَلَاةُ الْاِسْتِخَارَة

This *Ṣalāh* is offered to get Allāh's guidance on matters in which a Muslim cannot decide for certain the course of action. You are required to say a two rak'ah *Ṣalāh* after *'Ishā'* before going to bed. This is a *Sunnah* of Prophet *Muḥammad* (Pbuh). The process is exactly the same as any two rak'ah *Ṣalāh* except that you recite the following Du'ā' after the *Ṣalāh* :

اَللّٰهُمَّ إِنِّيْ أَسْتَخِيْرُكَ بِعِلْمِكَ وَأَسْتَقْدِرُكَ بِقُدْرَتِكَ ، وَأَسْأَلُكَ
مِنْ فَضْلِكَ الْعَظِيْمِ فَإِنَّكَ تَقْدِرُ وَلَا أَقْدِرُ وَتَعْلَمُ وَلَا أَعْلَمُ
وَأَنْتَ عَلَّامُ الْغُيُوْبِ ، اَللّٰهُمَّ إِنْ كُنْتَ تَعْلَمُ أَنَّ هٰذَا الْأَمْرَ
خَيْرٌ لِّيْ فِيْ دِيْنِيْ وَمَعَاشِيْ وَعَاقِبَةِ أَمْرِيْ فَاقْدُرْهُ لِيْ وَيَسِّرْهُ لِيْ
ثُمَّ بَارِكْ لِيْ فِيْهِ ، وَإِنْ كُنْتَ تَعْلَمُ أَنَّ هٰذَا الْأَمْرَ شَرٌّ لِّيْ فِيْ
دِيْنِيْ وَمَعَاشِيْ وَعَاقِبَةِ أَمْرِيْ فَاصْرِفْهُ عَنِّيْ وَاصْرِفْنِيْ عَنْهُ
وَاقْدُرْ لِيَ الْخَيْرَ حَيْثُ كَانَ ثُمَّ أَرْضِنِيْ بِهٖ ۔

Allāhumma innī astakhīruka bi 'ilmika wa astaqdiruka bi qudratika, wa as'aluka min fadlikal 'aẓīm, fā innaka taqdiru wa lā aqdiru wa ta'lamu wa lā a'lamu wa anta 'allāmul ghuyub. Allāhumma in kunta ta'lamu anna hādhal amra khairulli fi dīnī wa ma'āshi wa 'āqibati amrī faqduruhu lī wa yassirhu lī thumma bārik lī fīhī, wa in kunta ta'lamu anna hadhal amra sharrul lī fi dīnī wa ma'āshi wa 'āqibati amrī fasrifhu 'annī wa asrifnī 'anhu waqdur lī al Khaira ḥaithu kāna thumma arḍinībihī.

O Allāh, I seek your guidance through your knowledge and ability, through your power and beg of your infinite bounty; for you have power and I have none. You know and I know not; and You are the knower of hidden things. O Allāh, if in your knowledge this matter is good for my faith, for my livelihood and for the outcome of my affairs, then decide it for me and make it easy for me and bless me therein; but if in your knowledge this matter is bad for my faith, for my livelihood and for the outcome of my affairs, then turn it away from me, and turn me away therefrom, and decide for me the good wherever it be, and cause me to be pleased therewith.

Qaḍā' of Aṣ-Ṣalāh صَلَاةُ الْقَضَاءِ

We must make every effort to say our *Ṣalāh* at the set times. But if, because of unavoidable circumstances (e.g. forgetfulness, sleep), we are unable to say our *Ṣalāh* on time, we must make up for it afterwards. The *Farḍ Ṣalāh* is our compulsory duty to Allāh and we must make up for the missed *Farḍ Ṣalāh* whenever possible. The missed *Ṣalāh* when offered afterwards is called *Ṣalātul Qaḍā'*.

Lessons of Aṣ-Ṣalāh فَضَائِلُ الصَّلَاة

Ṣalāh is the most important of the five basic duties of Islām after Ash-Shahādah. We come closer to Allāh by performing it regularly, correctly and with full awareness of its significance and meaning. At this stage, refresh your memory about the purpose of our creation and the need for performing Islamic duties. Allāh has created us to worship Him. He says in the *Qur'ān : "Indeed I created jinn and human beings for no other purpose but to worship me."* (Sūrat-udh-Dhāriyāt 51 : 56) So, whatever duty we carry out, we must bear in mind that we are doing it for Allāh's sake. Only then can we expect to gain the desired benefits of the performance of *Ṣalāh*.

Allāh says in the *Qur'ān : "Successful indeed are the believers who are humble in prayers."* (Sūratul Mu'minūn 23 : 1-2)

Prophet *Muḥammad* (Pbuh) said : "The five set prayers may be compared to a stream of fresh water flowing in front of your house, into which you plunge five times each day. Do you think that you would leave any dirt on your body?" When his companions replied, "None at all!", the Prophet said, "Indeed the five prayers remove sins, just as water removes dirt." (Saḥiḥ Muslim)

The lessons of *Aṣ-Ṣalāh* are :

1 *It brings men and women closer to Allāh.*
2 *It keeps human beings away from indecent, shameful and forbidden activities.*
3 *It is a training programme designed to control evil desires and passions.*
4 *It purifies the heart, develops the mind and comforts the soul.*
5 *It is a constant reminder of Allāh and His greatness.*
6 *It develops discipline and will power.*
7 *It is a guide to the most upright way of life.*
8 *It is a proof of true equality, solid unity and universal brotherhood.*
9 *It is the source of patience, courage, hope and confidence.*
10 *It is a means of cleanliness, purity and punctuality.*
11 *It develops gratitude, humility and refinement.*
12 *It is the demonstration of our obedience to our Creator.*
13 *It is the solid programme of preparing oneself for Jihād — striving one's utmost to please Allāh.*

If your Ṣalāh does not improve your conduct you must think seriously about where you are going wrong.

6

Eleven Sūrahs of the Qur'ān

إِحْدَى عَشَرَ سُورَةً مِنَ الْقُرْآنِ

(سُورَةُ الْفَاتِحَةِ وَمِنْ سُورَةِ الْفِيلِ إِلَى سُورَةِ النَّاسِ)

1 Al-Fātiḥah

سُورَةُ الْفَاتِحَةِ

بِسْمِ اللّٰهِ الرَّحْمٰنِ الرَّحِيْمِ ○

الْحَمْدُ لِلّٰهِ رَبِّ الْعٰلَمِيْنَ ○ الرَّحْمٰنِ الرَّحِيْمِ ○ مٰلِكِ يَوْمِ الدِّيْنِ ○
إِيَّاكَ نَعْبُدُ وَإِيَّاكَ نَسْتَعِيْنُ ○ اِهْدِنَا الصِّرَاطَ الْمُسْتَقِيْمَ ○
صِرَاطَ الَّذِيْنَ أَنْعَمْتَ عَلَيْهِمْ ○ غَيْرِ الْمَغْضُوْبِ عَلَيْهِمْ
وَلَا الضَّآلِّيْنَ ○

Bismillāhir raḥmānir raḥīm
Alḥamdu lillāhi rabbil 'ālamīn
Arraḥmānir raḥīm.
Māliki yawmiddīn.
Iyyāka na'budu wa iyyāka nasta'īn.
Ihdinaṣ ṣirāṭal Mustaqīm.
Ṣirāṭalladhīna an'amta 'alaihim,
Ghairil maghḍūbi 'alaihim wa lāḍḍālīn. (Āmīn).

In the name of Allāh, the most Merciful, the most Kind.
All praise is for Allāh, the Lord of the Worlds,
The most Merciful, the most Kind;
Master of the day of Judgement.
You alone we worship; and You alone we ask for help.
Guide us along the straight way —
The way of those whom You have favoured
and not of those who earn Your anger
nor of those who go astray.

2 An Nās (114)

سُورَةُ النَّاس

بِسْمِ اللّٰهِ الرَّحْمٰنِ الرَّحِيْمِ ۝

قُلْ اَعُوْذُ بِرَبِّ النَّاسِ ۝ مَلِكِ النَّاسِ ۝ اِلٰهِ النَّاسِ ۝ مِنْ شَرِّ الْوَسْوَاسِ
الْخَنَّاسِ ۝ الَّذِىْ يُوَسْوِسُ فِىْ صُدُوْرِ النَّاسِ ۝ مِنَ الْجِنَّةِ وَالنَّاسِ ۝

Bismillāhir raḥmānir raḥīm.
Qul a'ūdhu birabbin nās.
Malikin nās. Ilāhin nās.
Min sharril waswāsil khannās.
Alladhī yuwaswisu fi ṣudūrinnās
Minal jinnati wannās.

In the name of Allāh, the most Merciful, the most Kind.
Say, I seek refuge in the Lord of mankind,
the King of mankind,
the God of mankind,
from the mischief of the sneaking whisperer,
Who whispers in the hearts of mankind,
from among jinn and mankind.

3 Al-Falaq (113)

سُورَةُ الْفَلَق

بِسْمِ اللّٰهِ الرَّحْمٰنِ الرَّحِيْمِ ۝

قُلْ اَعُوْذُ بِرَبِّ الْفَلَقِ ۝ مِنْ شَرِّ مَا خَلَقَ ۝ وَمِنْ شَرِّ غَاسِقٍ اِذَا
وَقَبَ ۝ وَمِنْ شَرِّ النَّفّٰثٰتِ فِى الْعُقَدِ ۝ وَمِنْ شَرِّ حَاسِدٍ اِذَا حَسَدَ ۝

Bismillāhir raḥmānir raḥīm.
Qul a'ūdhu bi rabbil falaq.
Min sharri mā khalaq.
Wa min sharri ghāsiqin idhā waqab.
Wa min sharrin naffāthāti fill 'uqad.
Wa min sharri ḥāsidin idhā ḥasad.

In the name of Allāh, the most Merciful, the most Kind.
Say, I seek refuge in the Lord of the Daybreak;
from the evil of what He has created;
from the evil of the darkness when it is intense;
from the evil of those who seek to promote discord (malignant witchcraft);
from the evil of the envier when he envies.

4 Al-Ikhlāṣ (112) سُورَةُ الإِخْلَاص

بِسْمِ اللَّهِ الرَّحْمَٰنِ الرَّحِيمِ ۝
قُلْ هُوَ اللَّهُ أَحَدٌ ۝ اللَّهُ الصَّمَدُ ۝ لَمْ يَلِدْ ۝ وَلَمْ يُولَدْ ۝
وَلَمْ يَكُن لَّهُ كُفُوًا أَحَدٌ ۝

Bismillāhir raḥmānir raḥīm
Qul huwāllāhu aḥad.
Allāhuṣ ṣamad.
Lam yalid wa lam yūlad.
Wa lam yakul lahu kufuwān aḥad.

In the name of Allāh, the most Merciful, the most Kind.
Say, He is Allāh, the One.
Allāh is Eternal and Absolute.
None is born of Him nor is He born.
And there is none like Him.

5 Al-Lahab (111) سُورَةُ اللَّهَب

بِسْمِ اللَّهِ الرَّحْمَٰنِ الرَّحِيمِ ۝
تَبَّتْ يَدَا أَبِي لَهَبٍ وَتَبَّ ۝ مَا أَغْنَىٰ عَنْهُ مَالُهُ وَمَا كَسَبَ ۝
سَيَصْلَىٰ نَارًا ذَاتَ لَهَبٍ ۝ وَامْرَأَتُهُ حَمَّالَةَ الْحَطَبِ ۝
فِي جِيدِهَا حَبْلٌ مِّن مَّسَدٍ ۝

Bismillāhir raḥmānir raḥīm.
Tabbat yadā abī Lahabinw watabb.
Mā agnā ʿanhu māluhu wa mā kasab.
Sayaṣlā nāran dhāta lahab.

Wāmrātuhu ḥammā latal ḥaṭab.
Fī jīdihā ḥablum mim masad.

In the name of Allāh, the most Merciful, the most Kind.
May the hands of Abū Lahab perish; doomed he is.
His wealth and his gains shall not avail him.
He shall enter a blazing fire,
and his wife, the carrier of firewood,
shall have a rope of palm fibre round her neck.

6 An-Naṣr (110) سُورَةُ النَّصْرِ

بِسْمِ اللَّهِ الرَّحْمَٰنِ الرَّحِيمِ ۝

إِذَا جَآءَ نَصْرُ اللَّهِ وَالْفَتْحُ ۝ وَرَأَيْتَ النَّاسَ يَدْخُلُونَ فِي دِينِ اللَّهِ
أَفْوَاجًا ۝ فَسَبِّحْ بِحَمْدِ رَبِّكَ وَاسْتَغْفِرْهُ ۚ إِنَّهُ كَانَ تَوَّابًا ۝

Bismillāhir raḥmānir raḥīm.
Idhā jāā' naṣrullāhi walfatḥu.
Wa ra aitannāsa yad khulūna fī dīnillāhi afwājā.
Fasabbiḥ biḥamdi rabbika wastaghfirhu,
Innahu kāna tawwāba.

In the name of Allāh, the most Merciful, the most Kind.
When the victory granted by Allāh and the conquest come;
and you see people embracing the religion of Allāh in large numbers
then celebrate the praises of your Lord, and seek His forgiveness.
He is ever ready to show mercy.

7 Al-Kāfirūn (109) سُورَةُ الْكَافِرُونَ

بِسْمِ اللَّهِ الرَّحْمَٰنِ الرَّحِيمِ ۝

قُلْ يَا أَيُّهَا الْكَافِرُونَ ۝ لَا أَعْبُدُ مَا تَعْبُدُونَ ۝ وَلَا أَنْتُمْ
عَابِدُونَ مَا أَعْبُدُ ۝ وَلَا أَنَا عَابِدٌ مَا عَبَدْتُمْ ۝ وَلَا أَنْتُمْ
عَابِدُونَ مَا أَعْبُدُ ۝ لَكُمْ دِينُكُمْ وَلِيَ دِينِ ۝

Bismillāhir raḥmānir raḥīm.
Qul yā ayyuhāl kāfirūn.
Lā a'budu mā ta'budīn.
Wa lā antum 'ābidūna mā a'bud.

Wa lā anā 'ābidum mā'abadtum.
Wa lā antum 'ābidūna mā a'bud.
La kum dīnukum walia dīn.

In the name of Allāh, the most Merciful, the most Kind.
Say, O disbelievers!
I do not worship what you worship;
nor do you worship what I worship.
I shall never worship what you worship.
Neither you worship what I worship.
You have your own religion and I have mine.

8 Al-Kawthar (108) سُورَةُ الْكَوْثَرِ

بِسْمِ اللَّهِ الرَّحْمَٰنِ الرَّحِيمِ ۝
إِنَّا أَعْطَيْنَٰكَ الْكَوْثَرَ ۝ فَصَلِّ لِرَبِّكَ وَانْحَرْ ۝ إِنَّ شَانِئَكَ هُوَ الْأَبْتَرُ ۝

Bismillāhir raḥmānir raḥīm.
Innā a'ṭainakal kawthar.
Fa ṣalli lirabbika wanḥar.
Inna shāni' aka huwāl abtar.

In the name of Allāh, the most Merciful, the most Kind.
Indeed we have given you the Kawthar (Abundance or fountain);
So pray to your Lord and make sacrifice.
Surely your hater is the one cut off.

9 Al-Mā'ūn (107) سُورَةُ الْمَاعُونِ

بِسْمِ اللَّهِ الرَّحْمَٰنِ الرَّحِيمِ ۝
أَرَءَيْتَ الَّذِي يُكَذِّبُ بِالدِّينِ ۝ فَذَٰلِكَ الَّذِي يَدُعُّ الْيَتِيمَ ۝
وَلَا يَحُضُّ عَلَىٰ طَعَامِ الْمِسْكِينِ ۝ فَوَيْلٌ لِّلْمُصَلِّينَ ۝
الَّذِينَ هُمْ عَن صَلَاتِهِمْ سَاهُونَ ۝ الَّذِينَ هُمْ يُرَاءُونَ ۝
وَيَمْنَعُونَ الْمَاعُونَ ۝

Bismillāhir raḥmānir raḥīm.
Ara 'ital ladhī yukadhdhibu biddīn.
Fadhālikal ladhī yadu'ul yatīm.
Wa lāyaḥuḍḍu 'alā ṭa'āmil miskin.

Fawailul lil muṣallīn.
Alladhīna hum 'an ṣalātihim sāhūn.
Alladhīna hum yurā'wūn.
wayamna'ūnal mā'ūn.

In the name of Allāh, the most Merciful, the most Kind.
Have you seen him who denies the judgement?
It is he who harshly repels the orphan
and does not urge others to feed the needy.
Woe to those who pray
but are heedless of their prayers;
who put on a show of piety
but refuse to give even the smallest help to others.

10 Quraish (106)

سُورَةُ قُرَيْش

بِسْمِ اللّٰهِ الرَّحْمٰنِ الرَّحِيْمِ ۝
لِاِيْلٰفِ قُرَيْشٍ ۝ اِلٰفِهِمْ رِحْلَةَ الشِّتَآءِ وَالصَّيْفِ ۝ فَلْيَعْبُدُوْا
رَبَّ هٰذَا الْبَيْتِ ۝ الَّذِيْٓ اَطْعَمَهُمْ مِّنْ جُوْعٍ ۙ وَّاٰمَنَهُمْ مِّنْ خَوْفٍ ۝

Bismillāhir raḥmānir raḥīm.
Li īlāfi quraish.
Īlāfi him riḥlatash-shitā'i waṣ ṣaīf.
Falya'budū rabba hādhāl baīt.
Alladhī 'at'amahum min ju'in,
Wa āmanahum min khawf.

In the name of Allāh, the most Merciful, the most Kind.
For the tradition of the Quraish :
their tradition of travelling in winter and summer.
Let them worship the Lord of this house,
Who provides them with food lest they
should go hungry, and with security
lest they should live in fear.

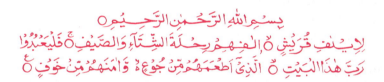

11 Al-Fīl (105)

سُورَةُ الفِيلِ

بِسْمِ اللّٰهِ الرَّحْمٰنِ الرَّحِيمِ

أَلَمْ تَرَ كَيْفَ فَعَلَ رَبُّكَ بِأَصْحٰبِ الْفِيلِ ۝ أَلَمْ يَجْعَلْ كَيْدَهُمْ
فِي تَضْلِيلٍ ۝ وَأَرْسَلَ عَلَيْهِمْ طَيْرًا أَبَابِيلَ ۝ تَرْمِيهِمْ بِحِجَارَةٍ
مِنْ سِجِّيلٍ ۝ فَجَعَلَهُمْ كَعَصْفٍ مَأْكُولٍ ۝

Bismillāhir raḥmānir raḥīm.
Alam tara kaifa fa'ala rabbuka bi aṣḥābil fīl.
Alam yaj'al kaidahum fi taḍlīl.
Wa arsala 'alaihim ṭairān abābīl.
Tarmīhim biḥijāratim min sijjīl
Fa ja'alahum ka'aṣfim ma'kūl.

In the name of Allāh, the most Merciful, the most Kind.
Have you not seen how your Lord has
dealt with the people of the elephant?
Did he not cause their treacherous plan to be futile,
and send against them flights of birds,
which pelted them with stones of sand and clay?
Thus He made them like devoured dry leaves.

Selected Qur'ānic verses on Ma'rūf and Munkar

بَعْضُ الْآيَاتِ الْمُخْتَارَةِ مِنَ الْقُرْآنِ الْكَرِيمِ
فِي الْأَمْرِ بِالْمَعْرُوفِ وَالنَّهْيِ عَنِ الْمُنْكَرِ

Ma'rūf   اَلْمَعْرُوف

1. وَأْمُرْ بِالْمَعْرُوفِ   *Wa'mur bil ma'rūf*
"*And promote what is good*" (Sūrah Luqmān 31 : 17)

2. أَقِيمُوا الصَّلَاةَ   *Aqīmuṣ Ṣalāh*
"*Establish Ṣalāh*" (Sūratul Baqarah 2 : 83)

3. ادْعُ إِلَى سَبِيلِ رَبِّكَ بِالْحِكْمَةِ وَالْمَوْعِظَةِ الْحَسَنَةِ   *Ud'u ilā sabīli rabbika bil ḥikmati wal maw'iẓatil ḥasanah*
"*Call to the way of your Lord with wisdom and beautiful expressions*" (Sūratun Naḥl 16 : 125)

4. وَكُلُوا مِمَّا رَزَقَكُمُ اللَّهُ حَلَالًا طَيِّبًا   *Wakulū mimmā razaqakumullāhu ḥalalan ṭayyiba*
"*And eat of that which Allāh has bestowed on you as food lawful and good*" (Sūratul Mā'idah 5 : 88)

5. وَاعْتَصِمُوا بِحَبْلِ اللَّهِ جَمِيعًا   *Wa'taṣimū bi ḥablillāhi Jamī'a*
"*And hold fast, all of you together, the rope of Allāh*"
(Sūrah Āli 'Imrān 3 : 103)

6. وَتَعَاوَنُوا عَلَى الْبِرِّ وَالتَّقْوَى   *Wata 'āwanū 'alal birri wat taqwā*
"*And help one another in righteousness and pious duty*"
(Sūratul Mā'idah 3 : 2)

7 وَأَطِيعُوا اللَّهَ وَرَسُولَهُ ، *Wa aṭi'ullaha wa rasūlah*

"And obey Allah and His messenger" (Suratul Anfal 8 : 1)

8 وَتَوَاصَوْا بِالْحَقِّ ۙ وَتَوَاصَوْا بِالصَّبْرِ *Wa tawa ṣawbil ḥaqqi, wa tawa ṣawbiṣṣabr*

"And encourage one another to truth and exhort one another to be steadfast" (Sūratul 'Aṣr 103 : 3)

9 وَبِالْوَالِدَيْنِ إِحْسَانًا ، *Wa bil wālidaini iḥsāna*

"And be kind to your parents" (Sūratul Isrā' 17 : 23)

10 وَقُولُوا لِلنَّاسِ حُسْنًا ، *Wa qūlū linnāsi ḥusna*

"And speak kindly to people" (Sūratul Baqarah 2 : 83)

11 وَأَوْفُوا بِالْعَهْدِ ، *Wa awfū bil 'ahd*

"And keep your covenant" (Sūratul Isrā' 17 : 34)

12 وَلَذِكْرُ اللَّهِ أَكْبَرُ ، *Wa la dhikrullāhi akbar*

"Remembrance of Allāh is the greatest thing" (Sūratul 'Ankabūt 29 : 45)

13 قَدْ أَفْلَحَ مَن زَكَّاهَا *Qad aflaḥa man zakkāha*

"He is successful who purifies his soul" (Sūratus Shams 91 : 9)

14 ادْخُلُوا فِي السِّلْمِ كَافَّةً ، *Udkhulū fissilmi kāffah*

"Enter into Islām completely" (Sūratul Baqarah 2 : 208)

15 حَافِظُوا عَلَى الصَّلَوَاتِ *Ḥafiẓū 'alāṣ ṣalāwat*

"Guard your ṣalāh" (Sūratul Baqarah 2 : 172)

16 وَاشْكُرُوا لِلَّهِ ، *Washkurū lillāh*

"And be thankful to Allāh" (Sūratul Baqarah 2 : 172)

17 اسْتَعِينُوا بِالصَّبْرِ وَالصَّلَاةِ ۚ *Ista'īnū biṣṣabri waṣ ṣalāh*

"Seek help with patience and ṣalāh" (Sūratul Baqarah 2 : 153)

18 وَاسْتَغْفِرْ لِذَنْبِكَ ، *Wastaghfir lidhambik*
"And ask forgiveness for your sins" (Sūrah Muhammad 47 : 19)

19 وَتُوبُوا إِلَى اللهِ جَمِيعًا ، *Watūbū ilallāhi jamī'a*
"And turn unto Allāh together" (Sūratun Nūr 24 : 31)

20 وَرَتِّلِ الْقُرْآنَ تَرْتِيلًا ۝ *Wa rattilil qur'āna tartīla*
"And recite the Qur'ān calmly and distinctly (with attention to its meaning)" (Sūratul Muzammil 73 : 4)

21 أَنْفِقُوا فِي سَبِيلِ اللهِ ، *Anfiqū fī sabīlillāh*
"Spend your wealth in the way of Allāh"
(Sūratul Baqarah 2 : 195)

Munkar الْمُنْكَر

1 وَانْهَ عَنِ الْمُنْكَرِ ، *Wanha 'anil munkar*
"And forbid what is wrong" (Sūrah Luqmān 31 : 17)

2 وَلَا تَلْبِسُوا الْحَقَّ بِالْبَاطِلِ ، *Wa la talbisul ḥaqqa bil bāṭil*
"And do not muddle truth with falsehood"
(Sūratul Baqarah 2 : 42)

3 لَا تُشْرِكْ بِاللهِ ط *La tushrik billāh*
"Do not make partners of Allāh" (Sūrah Luqmān 31 : 13)

4 وَاجْتَنِبُوا قَوْلَ الزُّورِ ۝ *Wajtanibū qawlaz zūr*
"And give up telling lies" (Sūratul Ḥajj 22 : 30)

5 لَا يَغْتَبْ بَعْضُكُمْ بَعْضًا ط *La yaghtab ba'ḍukum ba'ḍa*
"Do not backbite one another" (Sūratul Ḥujurāt 49 : 12)

6 لَا تَجَسَّسُوا *La tajassasū*
"Do not spy on each other" (:Sūratul Ḥujurāt 49 : 12)

7 وَلَا تَلْمِزُوٓا أَنفُسَكُمْ *Wa la talmizū anfusakum*
"Do not insult one another" (Sūratul Ḥujurāt 49 : 11)

8 لَا تَقْرَبُوا الزِّنَا *La taqrabuz Zinā*
"Do not come near adultery" (Sūratul Isrā' 17 : 32)

9 لَا يُبْدِينَ زِينَتَهُنَّ إِلَّا لِبُعُولَتِهِنَّ .... *La yubdina zinatahunna illa libu 'ūlatihinna*
"The women should not display their beauty except to their husbands" (Sūratun Nūr 24 : 31)

10 لَا تَكْتُمُوا الشَّهَادَةَ *La taktumus shahādah*
"Do not hide your testimony" (Sūratul Baqarah 2 : 283)

11 وَلَا تَمْشِ فِي الْأَرْضِ مَرَحًا *Wa la tamshi fil arḍi maraḥa*
"And do not walk on the earth haughtily" (Sūratul Isrā' 11 : 37)

12 وَلَا تَنَابَزُوا بِالْأَلْقَابِ *Wa la tanabazu bil alqāb*
"And do not call one another by nicknames"
(Sūratul Ḥujurāt 49 : 12)

13 وَلَا تَقْتُلُوا أَوْلَادَكُمْ خَشْيَةَ إِمْلَاقٍ *Wa la taqulū awladakum khashiata imlāq*
"And do not kill your children in fear of poverty"
(Sūratul Isrā' 17 : 31)

14 لَا تُبَذِّرْ تَبْذِيرًا *La tubadhdhir tabdhīra*
"Do not spend your wealth extravagantly" (Sūratul Isrā' 17 : 26)

15 لِمَ تَقُولُونَ مَا لَا تَفْعَلُونَ *Lima taqūlūna ma lā taf'alūn*
"Why do you say that which you do not do" (Sūratuṣ Ṣaf 61 : 2)

16 وَحَرَّمَ الرِّبٰوا ط *Wa ḥarramar ribā*

"And interest has been prohibited" (Sūratul Baqarah 2 : 275)

17 وَلَا تَقْرَبُوْا مَالَ الْيَتِيْمِ ، *Wa la taqrabū mālal yatim*

"And do not be near to orphan's wealth" (Sūratul An'ām 6 : 152)

18 وَلَا تَعَاوَنُوْا عَلَى الْاِثْمِ وَالْعُدْوَانِ ص *Wa la ta'āwanū 'alal ithmi wal 'udwān*

"And do not help one another in sin and enmity"
(Sūratul Mā'idah 5 : 2)

19 وَلَا تَهِنُوْا وَلَا تَحْزَنُوْا وَاَنْتُمُ الْاَعْلَوْنَ اِنْ كُنْتُمْ مُّؤْمِنِيْنَ ۝

Wa la tahinū wa lā taḥzanū wa antumul a'lawna in kuntum mu'minīn

"And do not be of broken heart and do not grieve; you will win if you are firm believers" (Sūrah Āli 'Imrān 3 : 139)

8

Declaration of Faith : الشَّهَادَة :-

1 Kalimah Tayyībah : اَلْكَلِمَةُ الطَّيِّبَةُ

لَآ اِلٰهَ اِلَّا اللّٰهُ مُحَمَّدٌ رَّسُوْلُ اللّٰهِ

Lā ilāha illal lāhu Muḥammadur rasūlul Lāh.

There is no god but Allāh; Muḥammad is the messenger of Allāh.

2 Kalimah Ash-Shahādah : كَلِمَةُ الشَّهَادَةِ :-

اَشْهَدُ اَنْ لَّآ اِلٰهَ اِلَّا اللّٰهُ وَحْدَهٗ لَا شَرِيْكَ لَهٗ
وَاَشْهَدُ اَنَّ مُحَمَّدًا عَبْدُهٗ وَرَسُوْلُهٗ

Ash hadu al lā ilaha illal lāhu waḥdahu lā sharīkalahu wa ash hadu anna Muḥammadan 'abduhu wa rasūluhu.

I testify that there is no god but Allāh and He is one and has no partner and I also testify that Muḥammad is His servant and messenger.

3 Kalimah Al-Īmanul Mujmal : اَلْاِيْمَانُ الْمُجْمَلُ :-

اٰمَنْتُ بِاللّٰهِ كَمَا هُوَ بِاَسْمَآئِهٖ وَصِفَاتِهٖ وَقَبِلْتُ جَمِيْعَ اَحْكَامِهٖ

Āmantu billāhi kamā huwa biasmā'ihī wa ṣifātihī wa qabiltu jamī'a aḥkāmihī.

I believe in Allāh (as He is) with all His names and attributes and I accept all His Commands.

4 Kalimah Al-Īmānul Mufaṣṣal : اَلْاِيْمَانُ الْمُفَصَّلُ :-

اٰمَنْتُ بِاللّٰهِ وَمَلٰٓئِكَتِهٖ وَكُتُبِهٖ وَرُسُلِهٖ وَالْيَوْمِ الْاٰخِرِ
وَالْقَدْرِ خَيْرِهٖ وَشَرِّهٖ مِنَ اللّٰهِ تَعَالٰى وَالْبَعْثِ بَعْدَ الْمَوْتِ۔

Āmantu billāhi wa malā'ikatihī wa kutubihī wa rusulihī wal yawmil ākhiri wal qadri Khairihī wa Sharrihī minal lāhi ta'alā wal ba'thi ba'dal mawt.

I believe in Allāh, in His angels, in His books, in His messengers, in the last day and in the fact that everything good or bad is decided by Allāh, the Almighty and in the life after death.

5 Kalimah Raddil Kufr : كَلِمَةُ رَدِّ الْكُفْرِ :-

اَللّٰهُمَّ اِنِّیْٓ اَعُوْذُبِكَ مِنْ اَنْ اُشْرِكَ بِكَ شَيْئًا وَّاَنَا اَعْلَمُ وَاسْتَغْفِرُكَ
لِمَا لَآ اَعْلَمُ اِنَّكَ اَنْتَ عَلَّامُ الْغُيُوْبِ تُبْتُ عَنْهُ وَتَبَرَّاْتُ عَنْ كُلِّ
دِيْنٍ سِوٰى دِيْنِ الْاِسْلَامِ وَاَسْلَمْتُ وَاَقُوْلُ لَآ اِلٰهَ اِلَّا اللّٰهُ مُحَمَّدٌ
رَّسُوْلُ اللّٰهِ

Allāhumma innī aw'ūdhubika min an ushrika bika shaiyan wa anā'alamu wastaghfiruka lima lā a'lamu innaka anta 'allamul ghuyūbi tubtu 'anhu wa tabarra'tu 'an kulli dinin siwā dınil islāmi wa aslamtu wa aqūlu la ilahā illal lāhu Muḥammadur rasūlullāh.

O Allāh, surely I do seek refuge in you from making any partner with you knowingly; I beg your forgiveness for the sins which I am not aware of; surely, you are the knower of all secrets. I repent for all the sins and make myself proof against all religions except Islam and I accepted it and declare that there is no god but Allāh. Muḥammad is the messenger of Allāh.

Appendix I

Glossary of Islāmic Words and Terms

It is difficult to translate Arabic terms into English (or any other language), especially those used in the Qur'ān and the *Ahādīth.* A brief explanation of the meaning of the important Arabic words used in this book is given below:

Adhān	The call to *Aṣ-Ṣalāh.*
Aḥādīth	(Plural of *Ḥadīth*) Reports of the sayings, deeds and actions approved by Prophet Muḥammad (pbuh).
Ākhirah	Life after death. It includes the Day of Judgement and the never-ending life after death.
Al-Jannah	Heaven – the place of eternal bliss.
Al-Ka'bah	The first place built for the worship of Allāh, in Makkah. Also called 'The House of Allāh'.
Allāh	The proper name of God.
Arafāt	The plain where people gather during Ḥajj.
Arkānul Islām	The five pillars (or basic duties) of Islām.
Aṣ-Ṣalāh	The five compulsory daily prayers offered in a particular way at set times.
Aṣ-Ṣawm	Fasting in the month of Ramadan, one of the five pillars (basic duties) of Islām.
As-Sunnah	The example of Prophet Muḥammad (pbuh) in what he did, said and permitted.
Ash-Shahādah	Testifying that "There is no god but Allāh and Muḥammad is Allāh's messenger". The first pillar (basic duty) of Islām.
Aṣr	Name of the *Ṣalāh* after mid-afternoon.
Az-Zakāh	Welfare contribution – a compulsory payment from a Muslim's annual savings, one of the five pillars (basic duties) of Islām.
Darūd	Reciting *Aṣ-Ṣalāh 'alan Nabiyy* during *Aṣ-Ṣalāh.*

Du'ā'	A supplication to Allāh.
Fajr	Name of the *Ṣalāh* at dawn.
Farḍ	Compulsory duty prescribed by Allāh.
Ghusl	Washing the whole body for *Ṭahārah*.
Ḥadīth	(Plural: *Aḥādīth*) A report of a saying, deed or action approved by Prophet Muḥammad (pbuh).
Ḥalāl	That which is lawful (permitted) in Islām.
Ḥarām	That which is unlawful (forbidden) in Islām.
Hidayah	Guidance from Allāh.
'Ībādah	Translated as 'worship', it refers to any permitted activity performed to gain Allāh's pleasure.
'Īd	A day of celebration: *'Īd ul Fiṭr* comes after the end of Ramadan, and *'Īd ul Aḍḥā* during Ḥajj.
Imām	The person who leads prayer in a congregation, or a leader.
Īmān	Faith or belief.
Iqāmah	The second call to prayer, made when *Ṣalāh* is about to begin in congregation.
'Ishā'	Name of the *Ṣalāh* at night
Islām	This is the name given by Allāh to the religion for mankind. It is a complete way of life. The word means submission and obedience to Allāh's commands to attain peace in this life and in the Ākhirah.
'Itidal	Returning to the position of *qiyām* after *rukū'*.
Jahannam	Hell – the place of eternal suffering.
Jama'ah	Congregation, when people say *Ṣalāh* as one group.
Janāzah	The funeral *Ṣalāh*.
Jibrā'īl	The angel (Gabriel) who brought revelation from Allāh.
Jihād fī sabīlillāh	Striving to establish *Ma'ruf* and remove *Munkar* from society, to gain Allāh's pleasure.
Jinn	Allāh's creatures created from smokeless fire with free will.

Kafir	A person who does not believe in Islām.
Khuṭbah	The sermon given before *Salātul Jumu'ah*. Usually a lecture about Islām.
Ma'ruf	Right actions. It's opposite is *Munkar* (wrong).
Maghrib	Name of the *Ṣalāh* just after sunset.
Mu'adhdhin	The person who calls the *Adhān*.
Muslim	A person who freely and consciously accepts the Islāmic way of life, and sincerely practices it.
Muḥammad	(pbuh) The final messenger of Allāh to Mankind.
Munkar	Wrong actions. It's opposite is *Ma'ruf* (right).
Musāfir	A traveller.
Nafl	Optional.
Niyyah	Intention.
Pbuh	Abbreviation of 'Peace be upon him'.
Rukū'	Bowing during *Aṣ-Ṣalāh*.
Qaḍā'	Making up for a missed prayer.
Qiblah	The direction towards *Al-Ka'bah* in Makkah to which Muslims face during *Aṣ-Ṣalāh*.
Qirā'h	Reciting the Qur'ān during *Aṣ-Ṣalāh*.
Qiyām	Standing upright in Aṣ-*Ṣalāh*.
Qunūt	The special *du'ā'* said during *Ṣalātul Witr*.
Qur'ān	This is the sacred book of Muslims, the final book of guidance from Allāh, sent down to Muḥammad (pbuh) through the angel *Jibrā'īl* (Gabriel) over a period of 23 years.
Qu'ūd	Sitting after prostration in *Aṣ-Ṣalāh*.
Rak'ah	A 'unit' of *Ṣalāh*, each *Ṣalāh* having two, three or four *rak'ahs*.
Ramadan	Ninth month of the Islāmic calendar, the month of obligatory fasting.

Sajdatus Sahw	The two prostrations to make up for a mistake made during *Aṣ-Ṣalāh.*
Salām	Turning the head to the right and left at the end of *Ṣalāh* saying *Assalāmu 'alaikum wa raḥmatullāh.*
Ṣalātul Istikhārah	A prayer for seeking Allāh's guidance on a matter.
Ṣalātul Jumu'ah	The special congregational *Ṣalāh* said at midday on Friday.
Sujūd	Prostrating during *Ṣalāh.*
Sunnah	Additional *Ṣalāh* practised by Prophet Muḥammad (pbuh).
Sūrah	A chapters of the Qur'ān (plural *Suwar*).
Ta'awwudh	Saying *A'ūdhu billāhi minash shaiṭānir rajīm.*
Tahajjud	Optional *Ṣalāh* between midnight and dawn.
Ṭahārah	To be clean and pure.
Takbīr	Saying *Allāhu Akbar.*
Takbīratul Iḥrām	Saying *Allāhu Akbar* at the start of the *Ṣalāh.*
Tarāwīḥ	The special *Ṣalāh* said after *'Ishā'* in Ramadan.
Tasbiḥ	Saying *Subḥāna rabbiyal….*
Tashahhud	The recitation after two *rak'ahs* and at the end of *Ṣalāh.*
Tasmiyah	Saying *Bismillāhir Raḥmānir Raḥīm.* Also called the *Basmalah.*
Tayammum	Dry ablution, performed without water.
Thanā'	Saying *Subḥānaka allāhumma…* after *Takbīratul Iḥrām.*
Wājib	Obligatory.
Witr	Literally means 'odd' (opposite of even), and refers to the *Ṣalāh* offered after *'Ishā'.*
Wuḍū'	Washing for *Aṣ-Ṣalāh* in a prescribed way (ablutions).
Ẓuhr	Name of the *Ṣalāh* just after midday.

Appendix II

Places where you can buy MET publications in the UK

Al-Hidaayah
PO Box 3332
BIRMINGHAM B10 9AW
Tel: 0121 753 1889
Fax: 0121 753 2422

Al-Huda Bookshop
76-78 Charing Cross Road
LONDON WC2H 0BB
Tel: 0171 240 8381

Al-Muntada Al-Islami Bookshop
7 Bridges Place
Parsons Green
LONDON SW6 4HR
Tel: 0171 736 9060

Al-Nasr Islamic Centre
10 Ledgers Road
SLOUGH SL1 2QX
Tel: 01753 550788

Al-Nur Bookshop
54 Park Road
LONDON NW1 4SH
Tel: 0171 723 5414

Bait Al-Hikmah
115 Henham Hall Drive
NEWCASTLE NE4 9XB
Tel: 0191 274 7540

Book Case
29 Market Place
HEBDEN BRIDGE HX7 6FU
West Yorkshire
Tel: 01422 845353

The Book Castle
12 Church Street
DUNSTABLE LU5 4RU
Bedfordshire

Book Centre
Express House
White Abbey Road
BRADFORD BD8 8EJ
Tel: 01274 727864

The Bookshelf
81b Park Lane
POYNTON SK12 1OD
Cheshire
Tel: 01625 859494

Brighton Islamic Mission
8 Caburn Road
Hove
BRIGHTON BN3 6EF
Tel: 01273 505247

Call To Islam
5c Alis Street
KEIGHLEY BD21
Tel: 01353 611875

Chistiah Book Centre
49 Milkstone Road
ROCHDALE OL11 1EB
Tel: 01706 50487

Daley's Bookshop Ltd.
1/3 Grove Terrace
BRADFORD BD7 1AU

Choudhry Fashion
266 High Street North
Manor Park
LONDON E12 6SB
Tel: 0181 470 7078

Dar Al-Dawah
32 Hereford Road
off Westbourne Grove
LONDON W2 4AJ
Tel: 0171 221 6256

Dar Al-Taqwa
7a Melcombe Street
LONDON NW1 6AE
Tel: 0171 935 6385
Fax: 0171 224 3894

East London Mosque Bookshop
84-92 Whitechapel Road
LONDON E1 1JE
Tel: 0171 247 1357

Eastern Importers
14 Taverners Road
PETERBOROUGH PE1 2JQ
Tel: 01733 34447

Hammicks Book Shop Ltd.
18 Wolsey Walk
WOKING GU21 1XU

Indian Record House
41 The Broadway
SOUTHALL UB1 1JY
Tel: 0181 574 4739

Interfaith Education Centre
Lister Hills Road
BRADFORD BD7 1HD
Tel: 01274 731 674

Islamic Book Centre
111 Alum Rock Road
BIRMINGHAM B8 1ND
Tel: 0121 328 2174
Fax: 0121 328 2174

Islamic Book Centre
19 Carrington Street
GLASGOW G4 9AJ
Tel: 0141 331 1119

Islamic Book Centre
29 Hatherley Street
LIVERPOOL L8 2TJ
Tel: 0151 709 2560

Islamic Book Centre
120 Drummond Street
LONDON NW1 2HL
Tel: 0171 388 0710

Islamic Book Centre
443 Cheetham Hill Road
MANCHESTER M8 7PF
Tel: 0161 740 3351

Islamic Book Centre
8 Forest Street
NELSON BB9 7NB
Tel: 01282 694471

Islamic Book House
179 Anderton Road
BIRMINGHAM B11 1ND
Tel: 0121 773 8651

Islamic Book Service
Birmingham Central Mosque
180 Belgrave Middleway
BIRMINGHAM B12 0XS
Tel: 0121 446 4157

Islamic Book Service
52 Fieldgate Street
LONDON E1 1DL
Tel: 0171 247 0689

Islamic Cultural Centre
146 Park Road
LONDON NW8 7RG
Tel: 0171 724 3363
Fax: 0171 724 0493

Islamic Dawah Centre
151 Balfour Road
ILFORD IG1 4HU
Tel: 0181 220 8611

Islamic Foundation
Unit 9, Old Dunlop Factory
62 Evington Valley Road
LEICESTER LE5 5LJ
Tel: 0116 273 4860
Fax: 01530 244946

Islamic Information Centre
209 Cricklewood Broadway
Cricklewood
LONDON NW2 3HS
Tel: 0181 208 1770

Islamic Relief Bookshop
314 Leeds Road
BRADFORD BD3 9QX
Tel: 01274 733375

The Islamic Society Cleveland
58 Virginia Gardens
Brookfield
MIDDLESBOROUGH TS5 8DD

Islamic Vision
481 Coventry Road
Small Heath
BIRMINGHAM B10 0JS
Tel: 0121 773 0137
Fax: 0121 766 8577

Kashmir Book Centre
523 Stratford Road
BIRMINGHAM B11 4LP
Tel: 0121 773 6634

The Khilafah Bookshop
238 City Road
CARDIFF CF2 3JJ
Tel: 01222 457356

Lancashire Council of Mosque
1st Floor
17 Holmrook Road
PRESTON PR1 6SR
Tel: 01772 463544

McGuigans Bookshop
40-46 Mill Street
NEWRY
Co. Down
Tel: 01693 66624

Madina Book Kiosk
14 Canford Road
LONDON SW11

Mizan Books
141 Berridge Road
Forest Fields
NOTTINGHAM NG7 6HR
Tel: 0115 942 2228

Mount Pleasant Islamic Trust
Purlwell Lane
BATLEY WF17 7NQ
Tel: 01924 465851

MSS Book Service
P.O. Box 59
MANCHESTER M20 9EP
Tel: 0161 448 1322
Fax: 0161 448 1320

Muslim Book Service
38 Mapesbury Road
LONDON NW2 3JD
Tel: 0181 452 9340

Muslim Information Centre
233 Seven Sisters Road
LONDON N4 2DA
Tel: 0171 272 5170

Muslim Printers & Booksellers
423 Stratford Road
Sparkhill
BIRMINGHAM B11 4LB
Tel: 0121 773 8301

RNB Enterprises
70 Queens Road
Walthamstow
LONDON E17 8QP
Tel: 0181 521 6380

Rolex Books
81-83 Wilmslow Road
Rusholme
MANCHESTER M14 5SU
Tel: 0161 225 4448

Rolex Trading Co.
6-8 Hallfield Road
BRADFORD BD1 3RQ
Tel: 01274 731908

Ruposhi Bangla Limited
220 Tooting High Street
LONDON SW17 0SG
Tel: 0181 672 7843

South London Islamic Centre
8 Mitchum Lane
Streatham
LONDON SW16 6NN

Southampton Islamic Movement
79 Winton Street
St Marys
SOUTHAMPTON SO1 1AL
Tel: 01703 233544

Subrung
131 Green Street
Forest Gate
LONDON E7 8JF
Tel: 0181 472 4146

Ta Ha Publishers
1 Wynne Road
LONDON SW9 0BD
Tel: 0171 737 7266

UKIM, Bradford
3 Byron Street
BRADFORD BD3 0AD
Tel: 01274 306299

UKIM, West London Islamic Centre
121 Oakland Road
Hanwell
LONDON W7 2DT
Tel: 0181 567 5898

Waterstones
(ordering service
at all branches)

West Side Bookshop
10 Sadler Street
WELLS BA5 2SE
Tel: 01749 676208

W H Smith & Sons Ltd.
(ordering service
at all branches)

Wipe (UK) / CRC Ltd.
409 Northolt Road
SOUTH HARROW HA2
8JQ
Tel: 0181 422 7786
Fax: 0181 426 8999

Zam Zam Bookshop
61 Brick Lane
LONDON E1
Tel: 0171 377 9813

Places where you can buy MET publications worldwide

Abul Qasim Publishing House
PO Box 6150
Jeddah 21442
SAUDI ARABIA
Tel: 00 966 2 671 4793
Fax: 00 966 2 672 5523

Aden International Trading
PO Box 8261
Falls Church
VA 22041
USA
Tel: 00 1 703 578 9644
Fax: 00 1 703 941 1815

Alefba Establishment
PO Box 3336
Abu Dhabi
UAE
Tel: 00 971 277 3075
Fax: 00 971 278 7780

All Prints Distributors & Publishers
PO Box 857
Abu Dhabi
UAE
Tel: 00 971 2 338572
Fax: 00 971 2 320844

Al-Serag Islamic Books & Supplies
6525 S. Gessner
Suite 2087
Houston
Texas
TX 77036
USA
Tel: 00 1 713 772 2421

Crescent Imports
PO Box 7827
Ann Arbour
MI 48107-7827
USA

Crescent Publishing House
103-43 Lefferts Boulevard
Richmond Hill
New York
NY 11419
USA
Tel: 00 1 718 848 8952
Fax: 00 1 718 848 8955

Dawah Book Service
1652 47th Avenue
Oakland
California
CA 94601
USA
Tel: 00 1 415 436 6422

Discover Islam
PO Box 10901
Manama
BAHRAIN
Tel: 00 973 536661
Fax: 00 973 533244

Halalco Books
108 E Fairfax Street
Falls Church
Virginia
VA 20046
USA
Tel: 00 1 703 532 3202
Fax: 00 1 703 241 0035

ICNA Book Service
100 McLevin Ave.
Unit 3A
Scarborough
Ontario
M1B 2V5
CANADA
Tel: 00 1 416 609 2452
Fax: 00 1 416 292 2437

ICNA Book Service
166-26, 89th Avenue
Jamaica
New York
NY 11432
USA
Tel: 00 1 718 657 4090
Fax: 00 1 718 658 1255

International Books & Tapes Supply
22-55, 31 Street
(2nd Floor)
L.I.C.
NY 11105
USA
Tel: 00 1 718 728 6108
Fax: 00 1 718 728 6108

INZ Books & Crafts
3419 Braeburn Circle
Arbour
MI 48108
USA

Iqra Agencies
PO Box 34027
Erasmia 0023
Transvaal
SOUTH AFRICA

Iqra Islamic Book Service
40 Purvis Crescent
Scarborough
Ontario
M1B 1H9
CANADA

Iqra' Book Center
6408-10 North Campbell Avenue
Chicago
Illinois
IL 60645
USA
Tel: 00 1 312 274 2665
Fax: 00 1 312 226 4125

Islamic Book & Speciality Shop
420A Canyon Oak Drive
Oakland
California
CA 94605
USA
Tel: 00 1 510 569 1679

Islamic Book Service
1174 The Queensway
Etobicoke
Ontario
M8Z 1R5
CANADA
Tel: 00 1 416 503 9197
Fax: 00 1 416 503 9197

Islamic Council of New South Wales
405 Waterloo Road
Chullora
NSW 2190
AUSTRALIA
Tel: 00 61 2 742 5752
Fax: 00 61 2 742 5665

Islamic Council of Norway
PB 658
Sentrum
0106 Oslo
NORWAY
Tel: 00 47 22 19 21 09

Islamic Dawah Centre
PO Box 4285
Cunupia Post Office
Cunupia
REPUBLIC OF TRINIDAD & TOBAGO

Islamic Foundation of Ireland
163 South Circular Road
Dublin 8
REPUBLIC OF IRELAND
00 353 1 453 3242
00 353 1 453 2785

Islamic Information Service
Darul Arqam West
Block 43
Jalan Merah Saga 01-62
SINGAPORE
Tel: 00 65 4713703
Fax: 00 65 7467006

Islamic Presentation Committee
PO Box 1613
Safat 13017
KUWAIT

Islamic Publications International
PO Box 247
Teaneck
New Jersey
NJ 07666
USA
Tel: 00 1 201 599 9708
Fax: 00 1 201 599 1169

Jerusalem Arts
9651 Bossonet, Suite 306
Houston
TX 77036
USA
Tel: 00 1 713 777 7071
Fax: 00 1 713 777 4418

Jordan Book Centre
PO Box 301
Al-Jubeiha
Amman
JORDAN
Tel: 00 962 6 676882
Fax: 00 962 6 602016

Kazi Publications
3023-27 West Belmont Avenue
Chicago
IL 60618
USA
Tel: 00 1 312 267 7001

Muslim Community Centre
4380 N. Elston Avenue
Chicago
Illinois
IL 60641
USA
Tel: 00 1 312 725 9047

Muslim Community Services Bookstore
1420 Harberson Road
Baltimore
MA 21228
USA
Tel & Fax: 00 1 410 744 7753

Muslim Information Network of Australia
5 Mena Court
Wheelers Hill
Victoria 3150
AUSTRALIA
Tel: 00 61 03 562 1798

NAIT Islamic Book Service
2022 East Main Street
Plainfield
IN 46168
USA
Tel: 00 1 317 839 8157
Fax: 00 1 317 839 2511

Saloojee's Books
PO Box 537
Lenasia 1820
Transvaal
SOUTH AFRICA
Tel: 00 27 11 852 2618

Sound Vision
843 W Van Buren Ste. 411
Chicago
Illinois
IL 60607
USA
Tel: 00 1 312 226 0205

WAMY
PO Box 10845
Riyadh
SAUDI ARABIA